Postcards
from the
Pug Bus

*The Continuing Adventures
of a Pug Dog Owner*

Postcards
from the
Pug Bus

*The Continuing Adventures
of a Pug Dog Owner*

Phil Maggitti

Published by Doral Publishing, Phoenix, Arizona
Printed in the United States of America.

Edited by MaryEllen Smith
Interior Design by The Printed Page
Cover Design by 1106 Design
Photo Credits: All photos by Phil Maggitti except page 80 (photo by Jeff Keefe).

Library of Congress Card Number: 2004101443
ISBN: 0-944875-98-X

For my wife Mary Ann, our pugs,
their veterinarians, and the many vets' children
we have put through college.

No animals were harmed in the writing of this book.

Contents

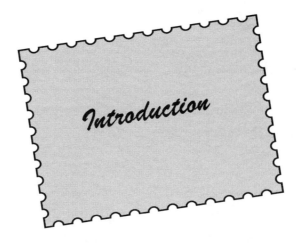

Introduction

There is no better way to breathe life into a career than by retiring. Like death, retirement is a great career move; unlike death, however, retirement does not have to be a one-and-done affair. The retiree still possesses options, one of which is to unretire—also a great career move. F. Scott Fitzgerald might have thought there were no second acts in American lives, but Michael Jordan, Richard Nixon, Phil Donahue, and a horde of wrinkled, aging pop singers who lived to hold another press conference have proven him wrong.

After pondering these examples carefully, I have decided to announce that this will be my last book. When the final galleys of *Postcards from the Pug Bus* go off to the printer, I am retiring from writing. There will be no sequels, no prequels, no *Return of the Pug Bus*—no matter how much an adoring public may clamor for more. Unless I change my mind.

Apart from the obvious leisure-time benefit, retirement has a large upside. It not only increases sales of the retiree's previous works but also entitles the retiree to mount the grand farewell tour, a dog-and-pony spectacle that garners florid accolades and, hopefully, expensive baubles the retiring artist may no longer be able to afford. Indeed, there is nothing more gratifying than a well-managed retirement tour—except, perhaps, a reunion tour.

Nevertheless, even though I am retiring for the first time—and as a virgin retiree am entitled to wear white on my retirement tour—I have chosen to skip the farewell turn. It's not that I have anything against receiving costly baubles. I am forgoing the victory lap because I don't like flying, meeting people, or being away from home for any length of time. Besides, my dogs would miss me.

In lieu of a retirement tour, I did consent to an exclusive interview with an award-winning journalist (AWJ), who agreed to speak with me (ME) on condition of anonymity. The transcript of that interview is presented below. It has been edited where necessary to avoid discussing topics covered later in this book.

AWJ: As you reflect on your twenty-one years as a writer, do you have any regrets about the direction your career has taken?

ME: No. South is as good a direction as any. The climate generally improves as you go, and you're never driving into the sun.

AWJ: Why did you choose to become a writer?

ME: That decision evolved from a canny attempt to grow into my limitations, which include an inability to function in groups larger than one, a disinclination to take direction, and a bedrock aversion to a nine-to-five schedule—or to any schedule, if the truth be known.

AWJ: Why have you decided it's time for you to retire?

ME: I made that decision in August 2000 when I was about to be wheeled to an operating room for a Sunday morning procedure that would remove excess fluid that had collected around my heart. Most people have a few ml of fluid around their hearts; for some mysterious reason that doctors were never able to determine, I had more than a hundred around mine.

Something told me the operation was serious. Why else would a surgeon give up an early tee time on a Sunday in August? As the nurses were steering me down the hall, I said to my wife, "If I get out of this place alive, I'm retiring." When opportunism knocks, I answer.

AWJ: What did you wife say?

ME: Like she was going to argue with me at that point? When you're flat on your back on a hospital gurney on the way to the operating room, you've got the world by the [tail].

AWJ: If you decided to retire nearly three years ago, why did you wait until now (June 2003) to announce your decision?

ME: Because art imitates infomercials, and I didn't have any new art to promote. I'd been too busy with various writing assignments to devote much time to this book. Eventually I realized that the only way to finish the book was to retire in stealth, take some time to write it, then retire officially.

AWJ: What sorts of assignments had you been working on?

ME: I had eight books published between 1993 and 1998, all of them animal related, and I helped to get a couple of pet magazines up and running between 1996 and 2000.

AWJ: *Postcards from the Pug Bus* is the second book you've written about pugs. Why did you decide to do another one?

ME: The sales of the first book, for which I didn't take a royalty option, were my main inspiration. What's more, the first book is a pet-care manual—one of those do-as-I-say-not-as-I-do affairs that is, by design, long on advice but short on anecdotes and je ne sais quois.

AWJ: Are you comfortable giving advice?

ME: I prefer giving orders or, occasionally, my blessing. I've always thought the best thing one could do with advice is ignore it. Besides, pug owners don't want for advice. There are ten how-to pug books currently available, and another five will be published in 2004. What pug owners need instead of all that advice is a reality manual that picks up where the training manuals leave off—or never bother to go.

AWJ: And where is that?

ME: A pet-care manual cannot adequately describe all the colors in the pug rainbow, nor can a how-to book properly convey the ecstasies and the agonies of living with pugs. That's why I decided to write *Postcards from the Pug Bus*. I believe a book of anecdotes and reflections will appeal not only to prospective pug owners who want to find out what it's really like to live with these dogs, but also to current pug owners who have mastered the arts of house-training and feeding and are looking for something interesting to read about their favorite dogs.

AWJ: What *is* it like to live with a pug?

ME: It's like living with another person in the house—a charming, innocent-looking, impish layabout who loves a good time, isn't shy about expressing opinions, and is always trying to shake you down for whatever it is you're eating. If you've never experienced the joy of watching a pug come to terms with the world and trying to bend the world to its terms, your life is poorer for want of that experience. Pugs are all wide, soulful eyes; flapping, velvety ears; and panting enthusiasm. They are fetchingly soft, unerringly cute, endearingly klutzy, unfailingly energetic, and damnably stubborn on occasion. They can coax a smile from your soul on the most grim, lamentable days; and when the sun is shining, they have a way of making you feel as if it's shining only on you. We would all do well to observe them.

AWJ: What have you learned from your observations of pugs?

ME: Three critical lessons come to mind: a moral compass is worthless indoors, inspiration begins with a nap, and a short memory makes for a clear conscience.

AWJ: And what have you tried to instill in your pugs?

ME: All of pug training can be reduced to two commands: "come" and "no." The rest is window dressing—a lot of "look, Ma, no hands." I can truthfully say that all my pugs come when they're called. They might not always pick up on the first ring, but if I persist, they get the message. They also respond well to "no," especially if I'm walking toward them—or standing right behind them—when I say it. That's good enough for me. I don't need to inflate my ego at their expense.

AWJ: What are the practical advantages of owning a pug as compared to owning another breed?

ME: Pugs travel easily and are accepted more readily in hotels or motels than many other breeds. Pugs won't eat a hole in your discretionary income. They don't require a lot of exercise. They can be washed quickly and allowed to drip dry, and best of all, because they're small, you can have more than one. No wonder they ranked fourteenth among the 150 breeds registered by the American Kennel Club (AKC) last year (2002, the most recent year for which statistics were available before this book went to press).

AWJ: Do all your pugs know their names?

ME: Yes. That's their only trick. Sometimes when we have company, I'll gather the dogs and say one dog's name. That dog will cock its head to one side and look at me quizzically. Then I'll say another dog's name, and that one will do the same thing. By the time I've called the sixth dog's name, they look like a mime troupe performing "How Much Is That Doggie in the Window?"

AWJ: That's impressive.

ME: It beats the hell out of trying to teach them to play "This Old Man" on eight glasses filled with different amounts of water.

AWJ: Do you have a set schedule you adhere to when you're writing?

ME: I like to be at my desk by three in the morning, sometimes earlier.

AWJ: Why so early?

ME: That's the premium part of the day; the pure, unfiltered, extra-virgin hours. Nothing's gone wrong yet. There are no interruptions. The phone never rings. It's like being at a resort after everyone's gone back to the city.

That state of grace lasts about two hours, but I can accomplish more during those two hours than I can during the rest of the day. Of course, the fact that I sometimes call it quits after two hours may have something to do with that situation.

AWJ: Why do you stop after two hours?

ME: Because the dogs are early risers, and as soon as they wake up, they demand a walk and breakfast. By the time we've finished those chores, the paper's arrived, the kettle's on, and distractions have begun to slither from beneath their rocks.

AWJ: What are some of the distractions that writers who work at home have to contend with?

ME: I don't know about other writers, but I have problems with the morning paper, the Internet, any number of restaurants, and the television we just installed in the kitchen, which is where the dogs sleep during the day and where I prefer to work once the sun comes up.

AWJ: Why do you prefer the kitchen then?

ME: Because I don't lose as much time walking to and from the refrigerator as I would if I were working in my office.

AWJ: How many pugs do you have presently?

ME: The current number is six: Hans, June, Burt, Harry, Dexter, and Fetch. We've had as many as eight.

AWJ: Did you choose "people" names for your pugs because they're child substitutes?

ME: No! A pug is nobody's stand-in. Anyway, I've always thought of children as dog substitutes—and rather poor ones at that. I arrived at this conclusion after teaching in junior high and middle schools for ten years.

AWJ: You also used to raise pugs. Did you raise all the ones you have now?

ME: No. Dexter and Fetch came from a shelter in Philadelphia. We raised the other four.

AWJ: Are there any differences between the four dogs you raised and the two you adopted?

ME: There are physical and behavioral differences. The four we raised—Hans, his half-sister June, and her sons, Burt and Harry—have shorter faces, cobbier bodies, and deeper nose rolls than the other dogs. That's because Hans and company all come from show stock and were bred to conform to the AKC's standard.

AWJ: How do you know that Dexter and Fetch don't come from show stock?

ME: You can tell by looking. We whelped and raised six litters of pugs, and the worst-looking puppy in those litters was to Dexter and Fetch what Catherine Zeta-Jones is to Lily Tomlin.

There are also, as I mentioned, behavioral differences between the "show" pugs and the other ones. Dexter and Fetch are the only pugs we have that are territorial. If we're out in the backyard and someone walks along the sidewalk that parallels the front of our house—a distance of 175 feet from the yard—Dexter and Fetch will run to the fence and bark. The other dogs wander around looking to see if any food has fallen from the sky.

AWJ: Do you think you'll have difficulty adjusting to retirement?

ME: I expect I'll take to it like a pug takes to spilled food. I'll read a lot, rent every movie in Blockbuster, download every music file on Kazaa, study Eastern religions and cosmology, and devote my spare time to restaurants, gardening, and trivia, which are the real business of living.

Chapter 1
Divine Intervention Strikes Twice

On a warm Sunday afternoon in April 1990, I was sitting on a hill-side in Lancaster County, Pennsylvania, watching a timber race, when God spoke to me. Because more people claim to be familiar with the voice of God than with timber races, I should explain that the latter are jumping races in which a horse and rider navigate a two- to four-mile course studded with a dozen or more imposing wooden fences that range from just over three to nearly five feet tall.

Equally imposing is the mindset of the timber race fraternity, which doesn't like anything to happen that has not happened before. In timber country, to heir is human, automatic teller machines dispense old money, and styles in hair and clothing haven't changed since the flowering of High Prep in the 1950s. I normally don't frequent that kind of scene—the sixties is the decade in which I am stuck—and most days I don't like anything to happen that *has* happened before, but I was on assignment that Sunday for a horse magazine.

The text of God's message was simple. She said, "Phil, you need one of those puppies in your life."

I wish I could report that "one of those puppies" was a pug. A writer couldn't ask for a more compelling line on a book jacket: "The author's heartwarming journey began that fateful Sunday afternoon when God told him to buy a pug."

God, unfortunately, works in mysterious ways. The puppies to which she was referring were four Labrador retrievers. They were on display in the back of a Chevy Blazer parked at the bottom of the hill on which my wife and I were sitting when God spoke to me, which was, to set the record straight, the first and only time she has ever spoken to me. I have heard other voices on other occasions, but I have never been able to ascertain their origins.

As soon as God had spoken, I turned to my wife Mary Ann said, "Let's go look at those puppies."

Next to God, my wife knows me better than anyone else does. In some ways she knows me even better, so I was not surprised when she said, "We've got a houseful of cats already. We don't need a dog."

Technically she was correct. We did have more than a few cats at the time, most of which I had acquired.

I was about to complain that it wasn't very sporting to intrude upon this discussion with facts when I remembered having read somewhere that a person doesn't mean no until she has said it at least seven times. Therefore, I suggested once again that we look at the puppies. Once again Mary Ann said no. Actually, what she said was "Are you out of your mind?" which I took to be a no. That's when I told her about God's message—which she took to be a yes.

My wife and I had been together nearly eleven years by then, and during that time I had never attributed any of my brainstorms to divine inspiration. When I wanted to press a point, I generally resorted to sulking, pouting, cajoling, badgering, or whining, but never had I claimed that I had a purchase order authorized by God.

We left the timber races later that afternoon with a ten-week-old black Lab female—the yellow Lab in the litter had been claimed already. In the thousands of years since dogs were domesticated and puppies were first offered for sale, few purchases have been more ill-advised. What I knew about Labs could have fit on the front of a greeting card, which is where I had done my research on the breed. Beyond that I hadn't given a thought to whether our lifestyle and a Lab's were compatible. Lifestyle? I thought Labs were bred to lie in front of a fireplace in a well-appointed den. What's more, I didn't own a collar, leash, crate, or even a can of dog food. I hadn't a clue what dog-proofing a house meant, and I didn't have a fenced-in yard or a fireplace. Apart from the parent who buys a puppy in a shopping mall to stop the kids' whining, this was the most reckless

Harry in the sky with turrets.

puppy purchase imaginable; but when God is on your side, the reckless seems reasonable.

By November of that year I was beginning to think that God had a warped sense of humor. The eighteen-pound puppy we had brought home from the timber races had grown, sometimes audibly, into a sixty-five-pound dog of whom I was fond but with whom I could not coexist. Unlike the Labs on greeting cards, lounging about placidly in red bandanas, our dog radiated more untamed energy than a nuclear power plant when half the supervisory crew is asleep and the other half is playing video games. She chased anything that moved and gnawed on everything that didn't. She lived to get dirty and to roll in decomposing flesh. She preferred stagnant puddles to her water bowl. She wielded her tail like a battering ram, laying waste to the contents of the coffee table and inflicting stress fractures on the legs of anyone in her path when she bull-rushed her way through the living room. The only means of keeping her from pestering us when we wanted to watch television at night was to take her for a marathon walk through the woods in the afternoon. That exercise left her too tired to hector us at night. It also left us too tired to watch television.

I was just about convinced that the Son of Sam *had* gotten his instructions from a black Labrador retriever when our vet told me about a family with 2.5 acres and 2.0 children. This family had owned a Lab for twelve years who died recently. Our girl, I quickly decided, would be just what the doctor ordered—for them.

Although I was happy to have regained control of the television set, the house was terribly empty without a dog in it. The departed Lab had left a hole in more than the living room rug.

The emptiness was especially gnawing because I work at home. I choose to do so in the firm belief that Sartre was right when he observed that hell is other people. Dogs, however, are better than people. A dog doesn't erect shrines to its children or grandchildren on its desk at work; a dog doesn't complain about its husband, wife, partner, or bad-hair day all the time; and a dog won't clog up your e-mail with dozens of lame jokes.

I wanted another dog, but rather than wait for a second message from God, I began reading up on dog breeds. I did so in secret at first, because my wife had informed me that we weren't getting another dog unless God spoke to her the next time.

The more I read, the more discouraged I became. Large breeds need too much yard and exercise. Small breeds are high-strung, yappy, bad for a guy's image, or still need too much exercise. I was beginning to suspect that my ideal companion animal was a Chia Pet, and that I'd have to get used to the idea of driving to the post office and the supermarket alone. Then one day as I was leafing through a dog magazine, I noticed a paragraph about pug dogs.

Pugs, I learned, don't need much exercise, they love food, and, come hot weather, they prefer the great air-conditioned indoors. "My soul mates," I exclaimed to my wife, who reminded me that no matter what dog magazines might say, we weren't getting another dog without divine intervention.

That intervention arrived in a bookstore near 57th and Broadway in New York on a cold day in January 1991. We were killing time between interviewing Paulo Gucci and having lunch with

Cleveland Amory. (I might as well drop the only names I'm qualified to drop in the first chapter and get them out of the way.)

As I was looking through a book, Mary Ann walked over and
said, "I think this is a sign." With that she held out a 1991 dog calendar, wherein the featured breed for January was a pug. I was
tempted to say, "How come when God speaks to you, she has to
show you a picture?" I nodded profoundly instead.

"You ought to call Charlotte as soon as we get home," said Mary
Ann.

Charlotte was the president of the Pug Dog Club of America at
the time, a position endowed with Godlike authority. We had
become acquainted with her by phone a few years earlier when
someone gave her a longhair Scottish fold kitten we had bred. Every
so often Charlotte called to let us know how the kitten was faring.
The last time she had called, right before Christmas, I told her that I
felt guilty about being the only person in North America who
couldn't get along with a Lab. She quickly recited half a dozen
annoying things that Labs are known to do, then she admonished
me to call her first "before you go and get another dog."

After I finished talking to Charlotte that night, I related the
details of our conversation to my wife, but she insisted we weren't
getting another dog until she had heard from God.

"That's not fair," I argued. "We've got an unlisted number."

"That shouldn't matter," said my wife.

The pug Charlotte sent to us, a nine-month-old, neutered,
fawn boy named Percy, was chauffeured from Florida to Pennsylvania in late January by a dog handler returning home from the
Florida circuit. We arrived at the handler's house with a crate in the
back of our Geo Storm hatchback. After visiting a while with the
handler and his wife, we thanked them for taking care of Percy then
carried him out to the car and put him into the crate. While Mary
Ann returned to the house to get her purse, I said idly, "Well, Percy,
how's it going?"

At that the little chap nearly came out of his skin. He began to
bark, whoop, and whine, leap up and down, and paw at the bars of

the crate. I feared he might declaw himself, so I opened the crate. He fairly leapt into my arms—all because I had known his name.

When Mary Ann returned to the car, I put Percy back in his crate. He was still so excited that he peed all over the crate before we got to the end of the driveway and was obliged to sit on my lap the rest of the way home. He smiled the entire time, looking up at me occasionally as if to say, "Aren't you happy God got it right this time?"

Chapter 2

The Antimother

I wouldn't be writing this book if my wife Mary Ann had not decided that our first pug, Percy, needed another dog for companionship. The chief element of canine companionship, of course, is mutual butt sniffing, and our six cats were of no value to Percy in that regard. Cats would not be caught dead with their noses anywhere near a dog's butt, and any dog who goes snooping around a cat's butt will soon be wearing an eye patch and a prosthetic lip.

When Mary Ann said that Percy needed another dog for companionship, she wasn't thinking of another pug. She was, in fact, partial to Cavalier King Charles spaniels, despite the fact that William F. Buckley and the Ronald Reagans owned Cavaliers. I, however, tend to amass things that I like. That is why I have one of the world's largest free music collections, courtesy of the Internet. That is also why we had forty cats and kittens in the house one summer. Fortunately, I have never liked children; otherwise we'd be living in a dormitory.

As soon as Mary Ann had said that Percy needed a companion, I replied, "Oh good. Let's get a female and breed some pugs."

Mary Ann was horrified. The memory of the summer of forty cats and kittens, although three years in the past, must have appeared closer than that in life's rearview mirror. I promised her she no longer had anything to fear from the Law of Unintended Consequences, and I was soon on the phone to our pug mentor, Charlotte, who had sent us Percy.

As luck and the progress of this book would have it, Charlotte had a nine-month-old female named Debby and a deal I couldn't refuse. We could have Debby free of charge if we agreed to show her a few times, breed her twice, pay half the stud fees and half the cost of raising the resultant two litters of puppies, and whelp and care for those puppies until they were twelve weeks old. Charlotte and her husband Edward would pay the other half of the breeding and puppy-raising expenses. They would also split the two litters with us. Mary Ann and I would get the pick of one litter and every other puppy in that litter. Charlotte and Edward would get the pick of the other litter and every other puppy in it.

As it was late in the spring of 1991 when this scheme has hatched—and already too warm to ship a dog by plane from Destin, Florida, where Charlotte and Edward lived—there was nothing to do but drive to Tampa to meet them and to pick up Debby, who was, we had been told, a little shy. Perhaps wanting to mask her shyness, Debby burst into our motel room that July afternoon like a velour-covered cyclone, charging at our stately ten-year-old Persian, Polecat, and forcing her to take refuge on the bed. We could see Polecat thinking, "I rode eleven hundred miles in a car for this?"

Next Debby turned her attention on Percy, who was too stunned to move. She sniffed his equipment and snorted dismissively; then, placing her front paws on the bed, she hopped up and down, huffing and puffing at Polecat, who couldn't have been more dismayed if a vacuum cleaner had sprung to life and begun menacing her (one of a cat's primeval fears). When Polecat retreated to the far side of the bed, Debby followed, propelling herself sideways around the bed with her hind feet while keeping her front paws on top of it.

Debby was too busy terrorizing the cat to notice when her former owners took their leave. Later that afternoon she dove gleefully into her dinner, but turned cantankerous when we put her into an extra-large carrier for the night. We had read in several training manuals that dogs feel secure being crated their first nights away from home, but the trouble with dog-training manuals is that few dogs bother to read them. Indeed, I sometimes wonder if the experts who write such books even bother to read them. I cheerfully confess that I have written more animal-training books than I have read, but that's another story.

At any rate, instead of retreating to the security of the far reaches of her carrier as the dog experts had said she would, Debby banged and clawed at its door and made these tiny, strangulated noises that sounded almost human. That was Debby—one part sledgehammer, the other pathos. Obviously, we weren't going to get any sleep that night or any other night unless she slept with us.

After we had transported the shy Debby to our house in southeastern Pennsylvania, she proved to be an irrepressible bad-hat of a dog. She chased the cats just to watch them run. She never let us cut her nails without making us suffer. She attacked Percy if she thought we were paying too much attention to him. She seldom let us eat in peace. She was wont to sneak upstairs to go truffle hunting in the cats' litter pan and to leave a truffle or two of her own on the rug to express her disdain for lower species.

She was, in short, nothing like Percy. Where he was nervous, she glowed with self-confidence. Where he was sweet, she was sassy. Where he was stuffy, she was a bowling shirt. Where he was timid, she was truculent. Where he played life close to the vest, she lifted her vest at the slightest provocation. In the five-and-a-half months that Percy had lived with us before Debby arrived—a time that Percy often referred to as the happiest months of his life—we had connected the dots of his personality and had arrived at what we thought was a realistic profile of a pug as a mannerly, unobtrusive type. Debby, we soon realized, was given to coloring outside those lines.

Debby was bred in February 1992. The dog to whom she was bred had been one of the highest-scoring pugs in the country when he was being shown and had sired many champions. We were eager to see what kind of puppies Debby and this celebrated pug would produce. Before we had a chance to find out, however, we discovered that the person who had formulated Murphy's Law—if anything can go wrong, it will—must have been a dog breeder.

Seven weeks into her pregnancy Debby began favoring her right hind leg. Our vet, after examining Debby, told us that she had a luxating patella—the canine equivalent of a trick knee—a genetic defect that occurs to a greater or lesser extent in most small breeds. Worse yet, Debby couldn't be operated on for at least six weeks— not until her litter had been weaned.

On April 20, Debby had three puppies—two girls and a boy. The first puppy, a girl, was an easy delivery. The second, a boy, was not. He didn't survive. We feared we were going to lose the third puppy also, and we probably would have were it not for the diligence of our veterinarian, who popped over at 4:00 A.M. to assist in delivering her. The puppy was stuck in the birth canal and was cold to the touch by the time the vet arrived. Undeterred, the vet somehow extracted the puppy and proceeded to shake the life into it, holding the puppy securely in both hands and swinging it up and down.

The vet's performance was nothing short of brilliant. In addition to trying to jump-start the puppy, she put her mouth over the puppy's face and sucked fluid from its nose and mouth. Grimacing mightily, the vet exclaimed, "Yuck," and spat the fluid onto the floor. As I was wondering if Nancy Reagan's vet spat on the bedroom floor, the puppy, another girl, began gasping for air.

After the vet had departed and we had cleaned the floor, we put Debby and her girls into the whelping box we had set up in the bedroom. Then we put our tired selves into bed.

Shortly afterward we discovered that Debby did not like children, an obvious shortcoming in a dog being groomed for the role of matriarch. We made this discovery as the sun was coming up, which is far too early in the day to be making discoveries. Coffee? Yes. Amends? If necessary. But discoveries? Not before midafternoon, thank you.

Debby announced her dislike for children with a series of indignant snorts. Squinting painfully in the direction of the whelping box, we saw Debby's large, luminous eyes peering accusingly over the top of the box. They clearly said, "Yo! I sleep with you guys. Remember? Why'd you shut me in here with these dwarfs?"

We told Debby it was not unusual for puppies to seek maternal attention, but she wasn't having any of it. We wondered where we

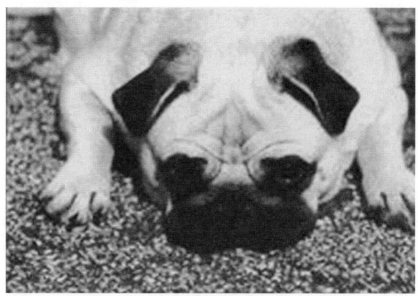

Debby's only failure as a mother was her thorough dislike of children.

might find ear plugs at 6:00 A.M. We hand-fed the puppies at 6:30. An hour later my wife, a university professor, left for work. Feeling guilty, I sneaked back to bed for a nap after I had fed the puppies at 8:30.

That evening we struck a bargain with Debby. The poor, abandoned puppies would sleep alone on their heating pad in the whelping box; and she would sleep with us, if she agreed to let the orphaned tykes nurse from her on the bed at the proper intervals. We, of course, would have to be awake at those proper intervals to oversee this arrangement—every two to three hours the first week, and every three to four hours for three weeks thereafter. She grudgingly consented, as long as we kept a hand on her while she was allowing the puppies to nurse, and as long as she didn't have to clean the little monsters.

The monsters' names were Patty (the first born) and Ella (the one who had been born half dead). We chose those names to commemorate Deb's luxating patella. Had the boy survived, we would have named him Luxor.

Freed from the rigors of motherhood, Debby spent her days in the backyard harassing the Doberman who lived next door. When we took her outside, Debby hobbled to the yard, her right hind leg bowed and wriggly; but when she spied the Dobe, she ran as straight and fast as ever. She raced back and forth barking at him like something possessed. She choked out imprecations while her short legs churned, her ears flapped, and her face radiated an intensity that was comical, satanic, and endearing. After she had stopped running, the leg was wobbly again, and she limped toward a shady spot to rest—but I never saw her wince.

Following what seemed like an eternal six weeks, Debby was operated on to repair her injured leg, to which the vet applied a splint. He recommended plenty of crate rest, but given Debby's aversion to crates, we ignored that advice. We were happy just to keep her from jumping onto the bed at first, and by the fourth and final week the splint was on, she was jumping onto the bed anyway.

We never bred Debby again, even though her daughters earned their championships in the show ring. Luxating patella is an inherited condition, and if you knowingly breed a dog that has produced such a condition, you knowingly participate in its advancement— to the detriment of your chosen breed, not to mention your karma.

Debby, of course, was pleased to be exempt from even limited maternal duties, though she never understood why we kept both her puppies. Surprisingly, she was more attentive to her grandchildren, two of whom still live with us, and to her great-grandchildren, two of whom also live with us, than she had been to her own daughters. She sought out her grandchildren and great-grandchildren and took much delight in washing them and cuddling up with them for naps. I was perturbed by this behavior at first, but then I remembered something that Socrates had once said: "If life sends you iron-willed dogs, you might as well make irony."

Chapter 3

One if by Hand

*The following story contains material of a graphic
sexual nature that may not be suitable for children
or for people of any age who are not professional
dog breeders. Parental guidance is recommended.*

Some concepts are so weird as to defy parody, so twisted to their core that they are almost too true to be good subjects for lampooning. Emeril Lagasse, Al Sharpton, World Wrestling Entertainment, and the dog fancy are examples of this phenomenon. Anyone setting out to mimic originals such as these is virtually obliged to omit their more outrageous tics for fear of being accused of exaggeration. This is why *Best In Show*, the movie that makes sport of "the sport of showing dogs," fails to reach the high-water mark on the lamppost. *Best In Show* does lift the rock (and the covers) off several of the more cheesy archetypes that populate "the sport of showing dogs," but some aspects of that "sport" are too curious for comfort and, hence, are not found in the movie. I am thinking specifically, though with some reluctance, of the aberrant practice known as artificial insemination.

On Valentine's Day 1992, our pug girl Debby came into heat, as do many human females on that occasion. The condition of being in heat, also known among laypersons as being "in season," is more properly called *estrus*, from the Greek word meaning "mad passion." In the majority of female dogs, estrus first occurs between ten and fourteen months of age. Male dogs, which, like their human counterparts, are always in heat, become sexually mature at roughly the same age.

Female dogs announce that they are in season not with a whimper but with a dark, bloody vaginal discharge and a swollen vulva. Despite these come-hither signs, females are not yet willing to accept a male's advances, nor do they ovulate right away. For the first six to nine days a female is in season—a period technically known as *proestrus*, from the Greek word meaning "I ain't givin' up the booty yet, sucker"—she is uncooperative or flat out testy if a male attempts copulation, no matter how tenderly he sniffs her butt or how often he pees on her bed.

> *Despite her Neiman Marcus breeding, we always suspected she had a Kmart soul.*

When the female's vaginal emissions change from dark red to pink, she is finally in true estrus, also known as a *standing heat*, from the Greek word that means "willing to stand for things she ordinarily wouldn't." If a female is approached by a male during this period, which generally lasts six to twelve days, she will raise her tail, swing it to one side, lift her pelvis, present her vulva, and get a look on her face that clearly says, "Get yer freak on, fool."

Ovulation usually occurs during a female's standing heat. After the eggs are released from the ovary, they have to marinate for seventy-two hours before they are ready to be fertilized, at which point they have only forty-eight to seventy-two more hours to live. In order to determine when that fertile period will occur, some dog breeders rely on tests involving blood samples or vaginal smears. Other breeders simply arrange to have their females mated on the ninth, eleventh, and thirteenth days after the first dark stains appear on the living room rug.

We scheduled a blood test for Debby at a reproductive clinic called C.L.O.N.E., but the gentleman we were supposed to meet there never turned up. Therefore, we resorted to the old-fashioned method, and on the ninth day after she had first "spotted," I drove Debby from our house in southeastern Pennsylvania to a well-known pug breeder's house to be bred. We bought Debby a white leather lead for the occasion. She didn't have much of a neck to put it around, but she seemed to like it nevertheless. Despite her Neiman Marcus breeding, we always suspected she had a Kmart soul.

The woman who owned the male to whom Debby was to be bred is an institution in the pug world, and I was somewhat apprehensive at the prospect of visiting such a holy site. Pug mecca turned out to be a stone house in a dated-but-still-monied neighborhood. The house looked much like the others on its quiet, leafy street. Nothing about the exterior of the house prepared me for the score of pugs living in the basement or for the life-sized pug made of sandstone lying on a bench in the vestibule. Indeed, I had started to engage that pug in conversation before I realized he wasn't about to answer.

A trifle chagrined, I rang the doorbell. There promptly arose from the basement a din that sounded like a posse of bristling voices riding across a blackboard. I heard someone bellow *Shut Up!*; then a pleasant-looking woman in her mid-sixties opened the door.

"We're with the party of the bride," I announced cheerfully.

She regarded me vacantly, then peered over my right shoulder. "I think the wedding is in a house down the street," she said. This being a weekday afternoon, I wondered if she was pulling my leg or if she was used to seeing people with pug dogs in their arms looking for a wedding in the middle of the week.

"I'm sorry," I explained. "I was supposed to bring this dog for breeding today."

"Oh," the woman said, still giving no indication whether she thought she or I was joking, "bring her downstairs."

I followed the woman through the living room, into a tiny kitchen, and down a cramped flight of stairs. As we started down the stairs, the din rose up from the basement again. Once more the woman bellowed the dogs into silence.

The basement stairs led to a ten-by-twelve-foot room that contained a lounge chair, a divan, a television, a telephone, a pair of end tables, and several large, wire dog pens. The walls were decorated with rosettes won at dog shows and pictures of dogs taken at various competitions.

"That's OK," I replied, not wanting to look like a prude. I couldn't imagine what could be so embarrassing about two dogs having it off.

"Sit down," said the woman. Still holding Debby, I settled into the lounge chair while the woman took up residence on the divan, which was also occupied by several pug dogs. A black Brussels griffon that couldn't have weighed more than five pounds and couldn't possibly have seen anything through the hair covering its eyes scrambled onto the lounge chair. Debby looked at the ragamuffin curiously. It aimed its face in her direction and panted. I concluded it was a male.

"Just put him on the floor," the woman said. I did and he scrambled right back onto my lap. His face was misshapen, and beneath all the hair he appeared to have one eye in the middle of his forehead. He also appeared to have a keen interest in Debby, who looked at him the way secret service men look at guys wearing a camouflage jacket and a Mohawk at political rallies.

After half an hour of small talk, the woman suddenly declared, "We might as well get this done," as if "this" was some distasteful household chore.

"Fine," I replied, and started to remove the persistent Brussels griffon from my lap so that I could get out of the lounge chair.

"You don't have to watch if you don't want to," the woman said.

"That's OK," I replied, not wanting to look like a prude. I couldn't imagine what could be so embarrassing about two dogs having it off. It wasn't the sort of thing I watched every day, but at least they wouldn't invoke the deity at any point in the proceedings the way humans that I have watched mating are wont to do.

I followed the woman into a small passageway. To the right was the doorway of a kitchen that contained several pugs, all females, who barked at Debby from behind a baby gate as if she were the new girl on the cellblock. At the end of the passageway was an eight-by-

Such a pretty face. Who would suspect her father was a turkey baster?

twelve-foot room in which five male dogs were confined in cages. When the dogs got a whiff of Debby, they began barking and hurling themselves at the sides of their cages.

"Pick me! Pick me!" howled bachelor number one.

"No! No! Me." pleaded bachelor number two.

There was a small table—about three feet wide and two feet deep—in this room. A pole on the left side of the table extended upward three feet, then curved ninety degrees and extended another foot to the right. A noose hung from the arm of the pole. As I was wondering what the noose was for, the woman nodded toward the table and said, "Put your girl on there."

I put Debby on the table, her head facing the noose. She looked as if she was wondering what the noose was for, too.

"It's OK, girl," I said, not entirely convinced that it was. The thought of two dogs table dancing in that confining space was puzzling, and I wondered why they weren't allowed to enjoy themselves on the floor.

> *Any illusions I had about the dogs breeding doggy style were banished when the woman got a small plastic cup and a rubber glove out of a cabinet drawer.*

"Put your girl's head into the noose," said the woman as she lifted one of the males out of his crate. He was panting furiously, and his tongue hung down to his knees. He reminded me of my high-school self in my father's 1955 Mercury hardtop trying to convince my date that I would still respect her the next day.

The woman plopped the male onto the table. He stuck his nose into my dog's business and began licking her as though she were Baskin Robbins' flavor of the month.

Any illusions I had about the dogs breeding doggy style were banished when the woman got a small plastic cup and a rubber glove out of a cabinet drawer. She donned the glove with a competence that said she was used to doing this sort of thing. Then, just as the words "holy shit" were forming in my brain, she thrust the cup beneath her panting male with her left hand and seized his shivering joystick with her right. With that she began tugging away on her boy like a dutiful high school girl in her boyfriend's father's SUV.

I couldn't believe my eyes. "This is probably against the law in some states," I thought, wishing that I had accepted the woman's invitation not to watch. Fortunately, there was a small television set on a shelf above the table; and I developed a sudden interest in the wisdom of Geraldo Rivera, who, I am sure, in all his journalistic adventures, had never come upon a scene as weird as this: a sixty-something woman waxing her dog's woody in a cramped basement in the presence of someone she had known less than an hour.

I am seldom at a loss for words, but this scene left me speechless. Happily it was brief, and the dog ejaculated into the plastic cup just as Geraldo was breaking for a commercial for a product guaranteed to "get out those stubborn stains."

The woman put the cup on a counter and removed her glove. Her dog, meanwhile, stood there panting. His member, hanging nearly to the table, reminded me of a huge tube of lipstick. I wanted to ask him if the assignation had been good for him—or to offer him a cigarette—but this didn't seem like the time for levity. Besides, his doghood looked so hideous I was afraid the woman had sprained it.

As I was wondering what the woman was planning to do with the contents of the cup, she whipped out a turkey baster from the cabinet drawer. She drew the contents of the cup into the baster and instructed

I wrote the woman a check for $300, which was the price of emission, and made a graceful retreat.

me to lift Debby's hind end off the table. She inserted the turkey baster where the sun does shine and squeezed its bulb, telling me to hold Debby at a forty-five-degree angle to the table for another minute or two to give the swimmers a chance to reach their goal.

When this bizarre ritual had been concluded, I returned to the sitting room. The woman continued to regale me with stories about the dog fancy while the Brussels griffon continued his assault on my lap. At the first lull in the bombardment, I wrote the woman a check for $300, which was the price of emission, and made a graceful retreat.

I drove cautiously all the way home, wondering if the people in the other cars could tell that the fellow in the minivan in the right-hand lane had just been an accessory to an act of bestiality. When my wife returned home from work later that day, she asked how Debby had enjoyed her outing.

"You're not going to believe this," I began.

Sure enough, she didn't. "That's disgusting," she said, looking at me as if she wasn't sure she wanted to be married to somebody who made up stories like that.

I finally convinced her that I wasn't kidding. Debby really had been bred by a turkey baster.

"In that case," said my wife, "you ought to give the woman an extra fifty bucks next time and let Debby enjoy herself."

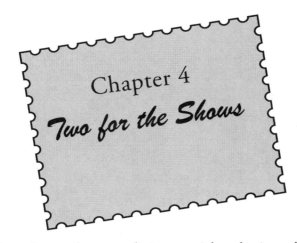

Chapter 4

Two for the Shows

A dog show is equal parts religion, social gathering, therapeutic exercise, declaration of self, and near-clinical preoccupation. I came to this conclusion after my wife Mary Ann and I had visited our first show, which was held in a pasture that had been tricked out to look like a cross between Woodstock and a colossal flea market. A number of large, open-sided, yellow-and-white striped tents decorated the field, which also contained several acres of motor homes the size of yachts, two dozen vendors selling all manner of dog paraphernalia from fine art to funny postcards, hundreds of people in L.L. Bean or office-party drag, and narrow car paths more congested than dirt roads in a Third World country at sheep-crossing time. The dogs being walked to and from the judging rings that late spring morning acted as if they had the right of way.

After parking our van, we trekked a heart-challenging distance to the show ring—a large square, actually, about eighteen feet on each side—where pugs would be judged. Pugs were scheduled for 8:30 because once the sun gets a leg up in the sky, even in early June, pugs who go walking are wont to seize up faster than a used car with a bad oil leak.

The exhibitors who were gathered near the pug ring had the hopeful look of stage parents at an early casting call. Behind a delicate veneer of civility and small talk, they sneaked sidelong glances at each others' dogs. I've seen witches in horror movies look more kindly on people they were about to impregnate with the spawn of Satan.

When the ring steward called for the first class, the dogs' handlers (some of whom owned the dogs they were showing and some of whom had been hired to show them) walked the dogs into the ring and proceeded to "stack" them in a row along one side. Stacking is the art of positioning a dog in such a way as to conceal its flaws from a judge at point-blank range. Pugs are stacked on the ground first, a routine facilitated by the use of bait, which is held a foot or so in front of and slightly above a pug's nose to keep the dog's attention after it has been stacked to the handler's satisfaction.

The bait used in this process is most often liver that has been boiled in gross amounts of garlic and salt until it makes the house smell like an abattoir. Handlers usually keep their bait in a jacket or dress pocket. A few handlers tuck bait in their mouths like a chaw of tobacco. When I saw one handler extract a piece of liver from her mouth then bite off a small piece to give to her dog, I was happy I had eaten a light breakfast.

After the pugs had been stacked, the judge, an authoritative-looking woman, walked along the line of contestants, looking studiously at each one as if trying to determine which of their number had passed gas. With an imperious nod, she then directed the contestants to walk the dogs around the ring until they had returned to their original positions.

Next the judge summoned each handler individually to stack his or her pug on a table—the better to have a hands-on look at that dog. After a pug had been examined on the table, the judge instructed the pug's handler to walk ten or so paces away from and then back to her. This is known as a down-and-back. It looked to me like a dress rehearsal for walking the plank. The judge then asked the handler to walk the dog ten paces away, turn left, walk another ten paces, then walk directly back to her. After each pug in the class had been examined and paraded, the judge ordered all the contestants to walk around the ring in a circle. As they were walking, she pointed to the winner of the class as if pointing to a lobster in a tank in a restaurant.

My wife and I had gone to this dog show because we would be showing a pug ourselves later that summer. On our way back to the van she said, "Are you sure this is something you want to do?" Her tone was one she reserves for my most *outré* schemes—like inviting an entire bar home for a nightcap at closing time.

"Ye-es," I replied, thinking that perhaps this wasn't the time to reveal that I wouldn't be the one showing our pug, an eleven-month-old female named Debby, whom we were getting in a few weeks on a breeder's agreement.

Some breeder's agreements contain more terms that the Treaty of Versailles, but this one was straightforward: we agreed to breed Debby twice, and to split the two stud fees, the litters, and the cost of raising them with the people who had bred Debby and were giving her to us. We also agreed to show Debby half a dozen times or so. Depending on her performance in those shows, we and her breeders would decide if she merited further exhibition. (A dog merits further exhibition if she or he appears capable of earning the points necessary to secure an AKC championship, but we needn't be concerned with the accounting process that underlies the awarding of that title.)

During the eleven-hundred-mile drive from our home in south-eastern Pennsylvania to Tampa, Florida, where we picked up Debby in July, I managed to coax Mary Ann into agreeing that she would cut a better figure in the show ring than I would and, therefore, she ought to show Debby. I don't know whether my accomplishment was a testament to my cajolery, to the fact that I had a captive audience, or to Mary Ann's genial nature. I've talked her into a number of things during our two decades of marriage, including sitting through a Rolling Stones concert in a football stadium during a northeaster, but talking her into showing a dog was one of my most difficult sells.

For Debby's and Mary Ann's coming out, I selected a show to be held in Great Barrington, Massachusetts, on a Sunday in late August. I chose this location even though there were other shows closer than a six-hour drive from our house. At that time Mary Ann's parents owned a summer cottage about twenty miles from Great Barrington, and I hoped that the chance to visit them would make up for the dog show.

As part of this devil's bargain, I agreed to train Debby. I hauled her out to the back yard each morning just after sunrise. We practiced "gaiting," the object of which is to persuade a dog to walk smartly on your left, neither lagging behind nor running in front, turning when you turn, stopping when you stop, and looking all the while as if she is happier than when she's rolling around in decomposing flesh.

After ten minutes had passed and no one had spoken to us, we felt like a pair of Crips who had strayed into Blood territory.

There should be nothing of the forced march in this performance, nor should the exhibitor look as if he or she is in a hurry to get to a rest room. Throughout the graceful promenade the exhibitor should keep one eye on the dog and the other on the judge while maintaining a look of confident aplomb. This was no easy feat to accomplish under the scornful gaze of several of our cats, who gathered at the bedroom window each morning to snicker at Debby and me. I suspect that a neighbor or two might have been doing the same.

In addition to gaiting we practiced stacking, both on the ground and on the picnic table. I spent so much time placing Debby's feet where I wanted them and getting her to hold her head at just the right angle that I began to feel like an assistant at Olan Mills during the month preceding first communion.

After several weeks of rehearsals, we were ready for Debby's debut. By *we*, I mean Debby and me. Mary Ann was about as ready as an innocent person on death row when it's time to meet the gurney. Nevertheless, we set out for Mary Ann's parents' place in Massachusetts the last Saturday of August, the day before the Great Barrington show. Debby had been bathed; her whiskers had been trimmed; she looked as pretty as a first communion picture.

On the way to the show the next morning, I reassured Mary Ann that showing a dog was just like teaching, which she does at a university. She replied that she didn't have to bribe her students with "disgusting bits of liver" to get them to sit still.

When we arrived at the pug ring, we felt as if we were crashing a party. Everyone seemed to know everyone else and to be sharing a secret to which we were not privy. After ten minutes had passed and no one had spoken to us, we felt like a pair of Crips who had strayed into Blood territory. We were relieved when Debby's class was called into the ring.

As I checked out the four other pugs in that class, I was sure we had the blue ribbon in the bag. To my expert eye the other dogs were too spindly, too long, too roach-backed, too crooked-looking, or some combination of the above. Debby shone like a silk purse among sows' ears.

After the judge had examined all five entries in the class, he sent them around the ring one last time. I smiled confidently. Our moment of triumph was at hand. Victory and a five-cent blue ribbon would be ours.

My smile froze when the judge pointed to one of the inferior dogs first. My smile turned to a grimace as he quickly pointed to the dogs to whom he was awarding second, third, and fourth places. When he had finished with all that infernal pointing, he still hadn't pointed to Debby. We were dead last in a field of five. If we had been a play, we would have closed out of town.

We slunk back to the van with our tails between our legs— except Debby, whose tail was bobbing over her back as she pimped for more liver.

"I put on stockings on a Sunday for this?" Mary Ann muttered.

"Don't worry," I said. "It's nothing that a little breakfast can't fix."

That was easier said than dined. The first restaurant we stopped at was filled. The second was, too. The third and fourth places we tried were closed. We weren't doing any better at finding food than we had done at finding favor in the ring. I was beginning to wonder if the judge's family was in the restaurant business. On our fifth try we found a place that had two empty seats at the counter. I'm not usually given to eating at counters, but we took them. Everyone stopped and stared at us as we sat down.

"What's the matter with these fools?" I thought. "Haven't they ever seen a woman wearing stockings on a Sunday before?"

After breakfast we returned to Mary Ann's parents' retreat. Her father must have forgotten about the dog show because he asked us how we had liked the Mass. I headed promptly toward the guest house and took to bed with the *Boston Globe*, consoling myself with the obituaries and Ann Landers. I didn't reappear until dinner, by which time I was hungry—for food and revenge.

Despite the unpleasantness at Great Barrington, I was able to convince Mary Ann to show Debby at two additional shows. At the first one, a mere hour-and-a-half away in New Jersey, there were five dogs in Debby's class. She managed to beat all but one of them. At the second show, two-and-a-half hours away in Pennsylvania, there were only three dogs in Debby's class. I figured we were sunk, though, because the dog that had beaten Debby in New Jersey was there, as was the gentleman who had judged that show; but the judge, in a dazzling display of creativity, placed Debby ahead of the dog who had beaten her the week before. Sadly, however, the dog who had been third the preceding week took the class. That's when I decided we needed a professional handler. Instrumental in that decision was Mary Ann's vow that she had participated in her last dog show.

We obtained the services of a professional handler, who, in nine shows, helped Debby to earn six of the fifteen points she needed for her championship. Her show career was cut short, however, by pneumonia, motherhood, and her luxating patella, which she developed while she was pregnant.

Even though I sometimes thought that showing dogs was an exercise in mass delusion without the special Kool-Aid, I had developed a thirst so powerful that after being diagnosed with type-2 diabetes and losing fifty pounds from fright, I decided to save us some money—handlers charge $50 and up for their services—and handle our dogs myself. By then we were showing Debby's granddaughter June, who was so attached to me that I had to hide when

Despite being vertically challenged, Burt takes his role as designated driver seriously.

anyone else showed her because if she saw me there was always the chance that she would race out of the ring to be with me.

After carefully selecting my show wardrobe from the local Goodwill—I hadn't worn a tie in years and I don't believe in spending more than eighty-nine cents for one anyway—I took the lead into my hands and stepped into the ring. I didn't do badly for someone with an aversion to dressing up. I showed June a dozen times and put eight points on her. I might have shown her more but for another incident in Massachusetts.

The scene of that crime was Springfield, about forty-five miles east of Mary Ann's parents' summer place, where we were visiting in July 1996 on the occasion of a family reunion. I slipped away from that gathering and took June to two shows in Springfield. We did reasonably well the first day, finishing third in a class of eleven or so, but close doesn't get you any points. The next day, in a class of

> *To say that I am a competitive person is like saying that Attila had a taste for contact sports.*

fourteen, we were dismissed with six other pugs so that the judge could have a closer look at the seven dogs she liked.

To say that I am a competitive person is like saying that Attila had a taste for contact sports. I am so competitive that my wife has played checkers with me only once. (She thought that my taunting her during the match then pumping a fist in the air and spiking a checker when I won was a mite over the top.) Understandably then, I didn't take too kindly to this latest judge's insulting decision. Nor did I take too kindly to the way I was dressed: pink-and-white striped seersucker pants, a white sport coat, a white shirt, and a bow tie. *A damn bow tie!* With my hair clipped unnaturally short, I looked like Pee Wee Herman on his way to a film festival.

As June and I walked across the parking lot toward the van, I threw the show catalog into the air, ripped off my bow tie and tossed that too; and then, diabetes be damned, I headed for the nearest KFC and ordered an extra-crispy chicken dinner, which June and I shared. When we passed a Friendly's a little later on the way home, I stopped for a double-dip ice cream cone and drove off into the sunset, never to be seen in pink-and-white seersucker pants again.

Chapter 5
Nothing Beats a Timex

East Otis, located in southwest Massachusetts at the foothills of the Berkshire Mountains, is the kind of place that can be seen only from the air. Some wags—especially those who enjoy a little night life, ethnic food, and a broadband Internet connection—have observed that the only way East Otis should be seen is from the air.

There is a reservoir, which everyone calls a lake, in East Otis. My wife's parents used to own a cottage—two cottages, actually—on that lake. We repaired to this compound several times every summer. The company was superb, the surroundings tranquil (except for the damn jet skiers), and dogs were allowed. Indeed, I could not say who enjoyed the lake more—Mary Ann and I or our five pugs—although they did grumble occasionally about the lack of good ethnic food.

All the dogs were curious about the lake at first, but none showed any interest in swimming and all seemed to know they shouldn't go too near the edge of the boat dock. Roughly twelve feet wide and twenty-five feet long, the dock extended over water about four feet deep.

One Saturday morning in June, when the water temperature was still too low for swimming, we took the dogs walking by the lake. They ventured onto the dock and were sniffing around when all of a sudden Hans, our youngest, who was just six months old at the time, did one of those things that are so stupefying they send time screeching into slow motion.

I was standing on the dock gazing idly over the water, contemplating a lunch-time visit to the fast-food trailer that sells clam bellies across the lake. Perhaps I should explain for the benefit of the food-impaired that clam bellies are to clam strips what aged provolone is to cheese food. In New England, where the Cabots (or is it the Lodges?) speak only to God, everyone speaks highly of clam bellies; and God, we are told, put bellies on clams for a reason: to make them taste good.

When she hit the water, she made the kind of sound that someone in the shower makes when someone else in the house turns on the water in the kitchen and the temperature of the water in the shower drops fifty degrees in a split second.

As I was saying, while I was contemplating bellying up to the fast-food trailer with the tourists, Hans went into a crouch. That's when time began to creep, as Shakespeare once said, "in a petty pace." Even though the interval between the time Hans went into a crouch and what he did next was less than a second, it seemed as if enough time had passed to drive to the fast-food trailer and back. For sure his life flashed before my eyes.

What Hans did next was to hurl himself in a perfect approximation of a belly flop straight out over the lake. We knew his vertical leap was impressive—we had the scratches on our kitchen door to prove it—but we weren't aware that his horizontal leap was equally impressive.

As soon as Hans had disappeared beneath the surface of the lake with a splendid *ker-splash*, time did the weirdest thing. It went from s-l-o-w motion to *fastforward* in a rush. Without giving a thought to my personal safety, I yelled, "Quick, Hon, Hans jumped into the lake."

By that time Hans had turned around toward the dock. His little legs were churning the water purposefully while his head floated on the surface like a huge muffin with two prunes for eyes. Hans, like many young pugs, had a touch of east-west eyes then; and the last thing I saw before his head disappeared beneath the

Hans' first venture into water was marred by his discovery that he didn't know how to swim.

surface of the lake a second time were the whites of his eyes, which were sweeping the sky like searchlights.

Mary Ann rushed to the end of the dock and began to remove her watch. "Quick, Hon!" I yelled. "He's going to drown."

Forgetting about the watch, Mary Ann jumped into the lake. When she hit the water, she made the kind of sound that someone in the shower makes when someone else in the house turns on the water in the kitchen and the temperature of the water in the shower drops fifty degrees in a split second. Only she made it louder. She also had this look of quizzical apprehension on her face that I had not seen since she approached the altar the day we were married. Meanwhile, Hans had come back to the surface of the lake to see what all the splashing was about.

Mary Ann seized that opportunity to lift Hans out of the water. I bravely took him from her and placed him on the dock. (Later that day, at the wedding we had traveled to New England to attend, friends of ours who own larger, more athletic dogs said we needn't have been so worried. Hans would have made his way back to shore on his own. At the risk of sounding argumentative, a risk I am frequently willing to take, I was obliged to tell them that it looked to me as if the only thing Hans was making his way to was the bottom of the lake. Did they think he was planning to walk ashore?)

After Mary Ann had emerged from the lake, she discovered that her watch was missing. The water being quite clear, we were able to make out the watch, a Timex, at the bottom. Somebody would have to go back into the frigid water.

I quickly volunteered to comfort Hans while Mary Ann changed from her sodden denim jumper into her bathing suit, put on diving glasses, and reentered the lake. Five seconds later she came up and handed me her watch. It was still running. I held it triumphantly aloft and said, "See, ladies and gentlemen, it takes a soaking and keeps on stroking. Nothing in the world beats a Timex."

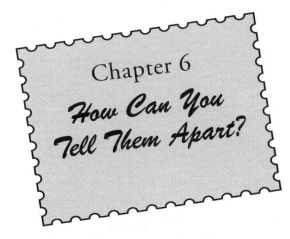

Chapter 6

How Can You Tell Them Apart?

I have often stood outside a supermarket, clutching a forty-pound bag of groceries, waiting for the crowd gathered in the parking lot near my van to disperse. The crowd—it's more a small knot of people, really—has been drawn by the antics of the five pugs inside the van, who are racing from one end of the vehicle to the other, bouncing off the seats, foaming at the mouth, barking like lunatics, and generally acting rabid, as they always do when strangers crowd around to gape at them.

Despite the fact that I'm waging a losing battle with gravity as I stand in front of the supermarket clutching my bag of groceries, I am determined to wait there until my Ben & Jerry's melts if need be, just to avoid acknowledging that these are my dogs and, worse yet, answering the questions that follow this admission. Sometimes I'm fortunate and there's a bench near the supermarket. I lurk there in relative comfort, trying to look as if I'm waiting for my driver to bring the car around, while avoiding eye contact with anyone near the van.

Of course, I could spare myself this wedgie if I didn't have a license plate that reads "Pug Bus" and a van filled with pugs that are inclined to go off whenever people gather to stare at them. Moreover, I don't imagine the "Rehab Is for Quitters" or the "Still Pissed at Yoko" bumper stickers on the van do much to deflect attention, either. Absent a water main explosion, an Elvis sighting, or a shootout in the supermarket lobby, a van with five pugs bouncing around inside is the reigning attraction in any parking lot.

I have never understood why the dogs go berserk when people approach the van. Unlike their owner, my pugs are not practicing curmudgeons who believe they have already met all the people they want to meet—and far too many people they didn't. Indeed, the dogs are not fussy about meeting people at all; nor are my dogs put off by

> *...few things in life are more tiresome than answering the same questions over and over.*

ill-advised hair, sequential layers of plaid, multiple body piercings, or an inability to accessorize—all of which can send me into a crippling depression. What's more, I'm certain that if I were walking the dogs—or walking one or two of them, as I never walk them all at once for fear of looking eccentric—and I met these same people, the dogs would fawn all over them; but let a pane of auto glass insert itself between the dogs and their admirers and the dogs begin snarling and snapping at one another, then turn on their audience, barking ferociously and spray-painting the windows with saliva. Instead of driving the observers away, this demonstration only serves to heighten their curiosity. Hell, I'd stare at that circus myself—and I'd probably solicit wagers regarding which dog was going to be the last one standing.

Nevertheless, there's a reason why I go to some lengths to avoid people who gather near my van: few things in life are more tiresome than answering the same questions over and over. That's why I gave up an unpromising career as a school teacher to pursue an even more unpromising career as a freelance writer, where the only question I have to answer repeatedly is "Where's the article that was due last week?"

A reluctance to answer the same question again and again is also why—among 742 other reasons—I do not have children. In short, I believe that each time you answer a question you have already answered before, you give away a piece of your soul.

Despite my battle-tested evasive maneuvers, I sometimes get caught with my groceries down. This happens most often when I don't look both ways before crossing the parking lot after the crowd gathered near the van has drifted off toward the supermarket. There I am, slinking across the lot like O.J. Simpson trying to slip into his house on a Sunday night, when an elderly couple or an endangered intact family or three ladies shopping together for greater efficiency

Friday night at the drive-in. From left to right: June, Patty, Ella (under seat), Harry, Debby (on front seat), Burt, Hans.

trap me as soon I set down my forty-pound bag of groceries and begin rummaging in my pockets for my keys, which are capable not only of shape-shifting but also of out-of-pocket experiences.

I've usually got my head lowered and am mumbling obscenities to myself at this point, so I don't see the second wave of pug spotters approaching. You'd think the sight of a furtive-looking man muttering obscenities would be enough to stop most people dead in their god-awful sneakers, but the slam-dancing pugs are such a powerful attraction I could probably stand there in a loin cloth with a bone through my nose and no one would notice. Therefore, just as I've tracked down my fugitive keys, I inevitably hear the first of several question-bombs bursting in air.

"Are they all related?"

"To whom?" I ask, raising the rear hatch of the van.

By now the dogs are hopping up and down on the back seat, facing me and my newfound friends. The more timid members of the audience take a step back, afraid that one of the dogs will hurl itself out of the van and sink its teeth into somebody's ankle. I'm tempted to claim that, according to the Centers for Disease Control in Atlanta, people are at greatest risk for pug dog bites when the back hatch of a van is raised in a supermarket parking lot. Generally, however, I save that remark for audiences with an obvious sense of whimsy—a quality in short supply around most supermarkets.

"Related to one another," says someone in the crowd with mock exasperation, the kind of mock exasperation that people use when they're trying to communicate with the terminally obtuse.

"Oh," I reply as obtusely as I can, which, on a good day, is somewhere between the obtuseness of your basic mall rat on Dramamine and a glue-sniffing elementary-school dropout. Then I add, "Yes."

…no matter how patient and exquisitely reasoned your answer to a question might be, someone is going to ask a follow-up question that clearly demonstrates he or she wasn't listening to you at all.

This is a carefully crafted response. When I taught school, I learned that an effective way to foster discussion was by asking open-ended questions—those that can't be answered by a simple yes or no. I trust, conversely, that an effective way to discourage discussion is by giving close-ended answers; but instead of squelching discussion, my yes elicits a follow-up question: "Are they brother and sister?"

Hoisting the grocery bag into the back of the van—and wondering if the nuts and chocolate boulders have begun rising to the top of my Ben & Jerry's Chunky Monkey—I explain that this dog here begat those two dogs over there and that one of them begat the dog trying to tunnel out under the seat and that the fellow whirling around in circles, barking as if he's got a bad case of Tourette's, isn't related to any of them as far as I know because "my wife and I adopted him from a shelter." (Mentioning a wife at this point is calculated to give the impression that I'm at least somewhat normal.)

Another thing I learned while teaching school is this: no matter how patient and exquisitely reasoned your answer to a question might be, someone is going to ask a follow-up question that clearly demonstrates he or she wasn't listening to you at all.

"Are they all yours?" someone asks.

"No. I belong to the Animal Liberation Front. I stole these dogs from a show, and I'm going to turn them loose in the parking lot as soon as no one's looking—which ought to be about next Thursday."

What I really say is, "Yes."

Then two people ask in unison, "Why do you have so many dogs?" and "How can you tell them apart?"

In answer to the first question, I sometimes say, "Because I can't afford an entourage." At other times I reply, "You can never be too thin or too rich or have too many pugs." I have to be careful with that remark, though, for fear of giving offense to persons who might be spatially overendowed or financially underwhelmed.

It's enough to make a person feel like Bill Clinton at the first press conference after his friendship with Monica Lewinsky became common knowledge.

The how-can-you-tell-them-apart question is a bit trickier, because pugs are, to the untrained eye, as difficult to tell apart as the members of an Amish family that has only six different people clinging to the branches of a five-generation family tree. I would love to say, "By counting the wrinkles around their butts, which are as unique as human fingerprints," but I've promised my wife that I wouldn't. Instead I launch into a discussion of nose rolls, ear sets, tail curls, and other matters that only a pug lover—or an Amish man at a barn raising—would understand.

No one appears to have a clue what I'm going on about, though one or two people nod their heads vacantly. They probably think I have some secret method of telling the dogs apart that I'm not willing to reveal—like counting the wrinkles around their butts.

By the time I've answered these questions, I've closed the back hatch of the van and have begun sidling my way toward the driver's-side door. The dogs, meanwhile, regroup on the front seats. Before I can get my key into the lock, someone asks, "Are they for sale?"

"No," I reply, thinking sadly that if I had left the dogs home, I'd be home myself now, sinking a tablespoon into the icy embrace of

Ben & Jerry's Chunky Monkey. My reverie is shattered by someone who wants to know what's wrong with their faces. It's enough to make a person feel like Bill Clinton at the first press conference after his friendship with Monica Lewinsky became common knowledge.

I want to reply, "They got that way from putting their noses into other people's business," but instead I say, "Wrong? What could possibly be wrong with a face like that?"

While my new friends are trying to come up with a response, I open the door, stop the pugs from escaping, and jump in nimbly. I tap the horn to signal my intent to escape, then drive away carefully as the dogs bark good-bye to their admirers.

Chapter 7

The Tie That Binds

The following scenes may contain material unsuitable for children under thirteen or for adults with a sense of propriety.

Many of us on the curmudgeon side of fifty can recall seeing dogs mating in public at some point during our misspent youths. In Chester, Pennsylvania, where I misspent my youth during the 1950s (I have misspent my adulthood in many other locations, including print), the sight of two dogs "having it off," as the British say, was always an occasion for ribald commentary and scurrilous insults directed at the families of the least popular, and usually smaller, members of our peer group—a group the nuns often referred to as "that bunch of hooligans."

Times change, however, and sometimes for the better. There are fewer dogs on the streets today than there were in days of yore (and "your mother"). In fact, there are so few dogs at large in most places that the chance to watch dogs mating in public and to make indecent comments while they do is, for better or for worse, no longer a rite of youthful passage. About the only folks who get to watch dogs mating with any regularity nowadays are the people who breed them. Could that be significant? Could it be that, contrary to all the pronouncements we hear about breeders dedicating their lives to improving their chosen breeds, the real reason people get into breeding is simply because they enjoy watching dogs mate?

Nearly forty years had passed between the last time I had seen dogs mating and the crisp November morning when I came in from a McDonald's run at roughly 6:30. All the dogs sitting around the kitchen table at my wife's feet, with the exception of Hans and Ella, came scrambling over to meet me at the door. Just then the tea kettle began whistling, and my wife Mary Ann started to get up from the table.

"Don't move, Hon," I said, sounding just like Hopalong Cassidy, a television cowboy whose name should be familiar to people on the curmudgeon, watching-dogs-mate-in-public side of fifty. "I think Hans and Ella are tied."

My first clue was the dogs' position. They were standing rump to rump at about a seventy-five-degree angle. My second clue was the fact that both dogs appeared to be mired in quicksand.

I took the tea kettle off the burner while Mary Ann put aside her cereal spoon and crossword puzzle to steady the virgin Ella and the equally virgin and somewhat perplexed-looking Hans. After a few moments, just as Hans' look was changing from perplexed to put upon, Ella released her hold on the lad and returned control of our lives to us.

"Hmmmm," I said. "I wonder if this is why people refer to getting married as "tying the knot.""

My wife did not answer.

"Or maybe this is why some guys say that other guys are lead around by their…"

"That's enough," said my wife.

Feminists believe that the personal is political. Writers, for their part, believe that the personal is publishable. Thus, after we had congratulated Hans and Ella on their excellent adventure, I sprinted to the computer. I realized that a person such as myself—who writes, among other things, books of advice for novice pet owners— had heretofore been remiss for not including, along with the standard instructions about house training, whelping puppies and the like, a few suggestions for passing the time while your dogs are tied.

Before I do, though, I should point out that according to James M. Giffin, MD, and Liisa D. Carlson, DVM, authors of *Dog Owner's Home Veterinary Handbook,* "the exact function of the tie is not known." Back home in Chester, Pennsylvania, we young geneticists

Hans and his muse, Leonardo, a mythical beast that is half lion, half statue.

said that dogs had to tie for a long time so that the bitch, a word we delighted in using, was sure to get pregnant. We also declared that dogs stood back to back while tied in order to guard one another against attack while they were waiting for the bitch to get pregnant, at which point she let the male go.

Giffin and Carlson, who have probably watched dogs mating only in laboratories, insist that "the length of the tie, beyond a few minutes, has little effect upon the likelihood of pregnancy or number of puppies conceived."

Without going into the anatomical precision necessary to explain how dogs manage to get tied, I should also note that Giffin and Carlson warn, "As the [tied] animals become frustrated and begin to tug against each other, the situation is aggravated. Do not throw water on the dogs or try to pull them apart."

No kidding! The only thing missing from that advice is the part that goes, "Needless to say…"

The aforementioned writers also neglect to tell us what to do while waiting for the tie to unbind. Hence the following suggestions, which are offered as a public service. Cut them out and tack them on your refrigerator door, even if you have to take down some of your kids' artwork to make room.

Try to recall some of the insults you hurled at the smaller, less popular members of your peer group if you used to watch dogs mating as a kid. One of my favorites was, "Is that your brother with your mother there? I didn't know he was out of jail."

Construct anagrams from the combined letters in your dogs' names. From *Hans* and *Ella*, for example, one can form *nasal heal* and *He's Allan*. If your dogs look as if they are going to remain tied until the cows come home, construct anagrams from the headlines in the newspaper.

Try to recall as many of the numbers associated with your personhood as you possibly can: your social security number, major credit card number(s), fax number, cell phone number, pager number, etc. Then try adding a few of those numbers in your head. My social security number adds up to twenty-seven. My phone number adds up to forty-four. My Visa card number adds up to somewhere around $1,500 a month.

If you have a catalog and a cell phone handy, go on a home shopping spree. If not, try to recall the second stanza of the "Star Spangled Banner." Or try not to think of an elephant for a full minute. Or mentally review the status of the persons who might be willing to buy a puppy from you. In addition, you might pray to the fertility goddess or have a snack.

Ours being the age of political correctness, writers should strive to create socially significant work. Therefore, I will close this treatise with some practical advice for those of you whose dogs remain tied after you have exhausted all the time-passing techniques presented above. Once again I cite the wisdom of Giffin and Carlson, who tell us that in order to separate tied dogs—if one of them is becoming agitated because he or she has suddenly remembered an urgent appointment elsewhere—"turn the male so that he remounts the female and then push on his rump to increase the depth of penetration. This relieves the constricting effect of the vaginal ring so that the dogs can slide apart."

Having been spared the necessity of implementing this close-encounters remedy, I simply offered Hans and Ella some Gatorade and a cigarette and put my Egg McMuffin into the microwave.

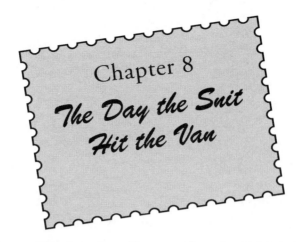

Chapter 8

The Day the Snit Hit the Van

Our pugs are like American Express: they don't think we should leave home without them. Most of the time I agree. The rest of the time I sneak out the side door.

Like all dogs, pugs have a well-developed sixth sense—the sense of travel—which enables them to read the signs of our imminent departures with an accuracy that ranges from the canny to the uncanny. The seat of this ability is the third eye, located in the Michelin chakra, a point that lies just above the nose break. The third eye allows pugs to transcend barriers of time and space. To do so, however, they need a ride; and that's where we come in, whenever we go out.

The pugs' delight in travel arises from their ability to live entirely in the present—a skill that humans foolishly traded for self-consciousness long ago. Wallowing happily in the moment, pugs don't give a thought to destinations. As a result they are the quintessential travelers, for if you don't care where you're going, one road is as good as another.

I wish the same were true for humans. Unhappily it is not, so when the going gets tough, the tough take a few pugs along to smooth out the ride. That is what I did when my wife Mary Ann and I set out for Glastonbury, Connecticut, one bitter February day to attend the viewing of our twenty-year-old nephew who had died of cancer.

Six solemn hours after we had left our home in southeastern Pennsylvania we arrived at the motel I'd selected. I don't know how people who travel without dogs choose a hotel or a motel—though

I suspect that proximity to museums, theaters, golf courses, and other cultural attractions might come into play. My choice of accommodations is always determined by two criteria: cost and the management's willingness to accept pets. Thus, for this funeral trip I had chosen, as usual, a motel that is part of a pet-friendly budget chain.

My choice could not have been more fitting. The motel had the look of death about it. I resolved as soon as we pulled into the parking lot that I'd never again make a reservation from a Web site that didn't post a photo of the "deluxe accommodations" being advertised.

The only thing strange about the room was the floor-to-ceiling mirror that occupied the entire wall beside the bed.

Because the motel was located in a post-industrial wasteland that looked ominous after dark, the only way into the place was through the lobby. I found this disconcerting because I had said we would have "two small dogs" with us, not four, when I made the reservation. (I didn't want the reservations person to think I was some kind of eccentric who travels with a lot of dogs.) Even more disconcerting was a sign next to the outer door to the lobby. Loosely translated the sign read: "This door is locked between 6:00 P.M. and 6:00 A.M. Anyone entering the motel during those hours must show a room key to the attendant at the desk."

Despite the straightforward tone of this announcement, I didn't have to worry about traipsing in and out with an entourage of dogs. The motel door was never locked; there was no one at the desk after dark; and whenever we passed through the lobby during the day, the person at the desk did not look up. I could understand this attitude. I didn't want to know what sort of people frequented that place either. What you don't see, you don't have to testify about.

These misgivings aside, I had to admit that our room was comfortable, spacious, and, given the circumstances—the snow and the subfreezing temperature outside—somewhat cozy. Of course, anyplace is apt to feel cozy if your fear of being mugged in the hallway doesn't materialize. The only thing strange about the room was the floor-to-ceiling mirror that occupied the entire wall beside the bed.

In view of the economies of scale and substance that characterize the decor of most budget motels that accept dogs, I thought the mirror a rather splashy extravagance.

For their part the dogs found the mirror diverting. They spent their first few minutes in the room snorting indignantly at the strange pugs snorting indignantly at them. That's a telling difference between us and dogs: we accept our reflections meekly even if they add fifteen pounds and an extra chin to our appearance, but dogs are inclined to challenge theirs.

I was still a trifle leery about leaving the dogs behind when we went to the viewing later that night, but Mary Ann, who is not given to paranoia as I am, assured me they would still be there when we returned. They were. So were those strange dogs in the mirror, but by then they had gone to sleep.

The next morning we awoke before dawn, as usual. After walking and feeding the dogs, we went out for breakfast. We had planned to stay two nights at the motel, but the Weather Channel was predicting a storm for the next day. Having tempted fate and escaped with our lives once, I suggested that the better part of valor consisted of checking out early, taking the dogs to the funeral and cemetery with us, and heading for home. The weather was cold, but not so cold that the dogs couldn't stay in their blanket-covered crates in the van for an hour or so while we were in church. If need be, we could leave the motor running.

Mary Ann, who enjoys the dogs as much as I do but who does not share my enthusiasm for taking them everywhere we go, acquiesced. She also agreed that the dogs seemed to know we were not our cheeriest and they had demonstrated by their unusually circumspect behavior—no unwelcome surprises on the motel rug, no madcap dashes out the door and down the hallway—how remarkably sensitive they are to their people's moods.

We returned to the motel, packed our bags, and made several treks down the hall, through the empty, unguarded lobby, across the snow, and to the van. On a couple of those treks, we encountered young women in high heels and party clothes leaving their rooms.

There were no dog shows that we knew of in the area, so we assumed these were "working girls" on their way home from the night shift. Consequently, we looked at each other and, achieving simultaneous exclamation, said, "That's what the mirror's for!"

The funeral, as solemn and sad as ever I want to see, was marred a little, I thought, by a priest who used words like *leitmotif* in his homily. I am more used to hearing phrases like "rough edges not-withstanding" or "could be a handful at times" in the sermons at funerals I have attended.

We emerged from the church into a bright and bitter landscape and made our way to the van. Our nephew Tim had decided to ride to the cemetery with us instead of his grandparents so he could catch a smoke. I, for reasons best known only to my dead Italian ancestors, was in possession of a pack of those gnarled Sicilian stogies that ought to have a skull and crossbones instead of a surgeon general's warning on the package.

When we opened the door of the van, it smelled, you will pardon the expression, like somebody had died in there. I almost said as much, but for once my tongue was restrained by my tactfulness. One of the two males traveling with us had had an attack of diarrhea. I'd always thought the term *explosive diarrhea* was amusing, but suddenly it had lost all its charm. The poor fellow had exploded out the front end of his crate. To this day I blame the water in that damn motel.

There was no way the three of us would have survived a ride to the cemetery inhaling those fumes. That would have been unsafe at any speed. There was also no way, or so I thought, we could get the van cleaned up in time to take our place in the funeral line, wherein we were driving third. Mary Ann, however, is used to cleaning up after animals, so she leapt into the van while I opened the back hatch to rummage for some paper towels and spray cleaner. Our nephew, meanwhile, stood decorously to one side. He appeared to be reconsidering his decision not to ride with his grandparents. Lighting a match in the van any time soon might have triggered an explosion.

The deluxe conversion model is equipped with a rear-passenger water bowl, privacy area, Oriental carpet, and a complementary bottle of Febreez.

After a few minutes of Keystone Cops maneuvers that involved getting the two males out of their crate, cleaning the van rug, wiping down the crate, then stowing the offending crate rug and soiled paper towels an a plastic trash bag in the back of the van, we assumed our place in the funeral procession.

No more than ten minutes from the church, before my nephew and I had finished debating the merits of cigarettes and Italian stogies, I heard my wife exclaim, "My God, he just shit all over my coat."

At that same moment eau d'diaper pail came oozing out of the back of the van once again, and worse came to worser when our nephew began gagging in the front seat. I started to cackle like someone who smokes twisted cigars on occasion while visualizing the gyrations we would have to go through to clean my wife's coat and the dashboard while trying to keep pace with the other cars, which probably contained nothing more unusual than somber-looking people dressed in black.

As I noted, Mary Ann is skilled at cleaning up after animals. Fortunately, her coat, a duster I had bought her for Christmas, is a black-and-tan houndstooth, ideal for camouflaging canine explosions; and her dress sported one of those neo-Victorian patterns much favored these neo-Victorian days, also ideal for disguising such eruptions. Even more fortunately, our nephew managed to keep his breakfast down.

Thankfully, the rest of the trip to the cemetery was uneventful. On our way from the grave site someone did mutter, "I wouldn't be in any hurry to get back to the car if I were you." A rather tasteless remark, I thought, considering the circumstances.

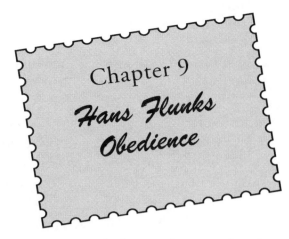

Chapter 9
Hans Flunks Obedience

The first time I saw an obedience class at a dog show I thought, "This has to be done with mirrors. There's no way dogs can be that well trained. It's unnatural."

I was particularly suspicious of the drill in which contestants told their dogs to lie down and then walked out of the exhibition ring, looking like pallbearers heading for their seats at an official state funeral. Having been a school teacher during one ill-starred period in my life, I knew what happened when teachers left their charges unattended: mayhem, mugging, attempted rape, and a rash of split infinitives.

I waited gleefully for the chaos to begin. A minute or two passed. The dog owners were nowhere in sight, yet the dogs lay precisely where they had been left. "They must be on Valium," I muttered.

Meanwhile, the spectators watching this performance spoke in deferential tones, the sort usually employed by people broadcasting golf matches on television. I didn't know about those dogs in the ring, but all this waiting and elaborate civility made me want to pee.

Another minute or two passed. The dogs were looking more and more like statues. Lot's wife, after that backward glance at Sodom, was more lifelike than those dogs. I began to get itchy, waiting for the first shoe to drop.

At last the dogs' owners marched solemnly back into the ring. They had been gone roughly five minutes, but those felt like the longest five minutes in human history. A few of the owners looked noticeably older, and I would have sworn enough time had passed for a person to get divorced and remarried in some states.

When the owners returned, I figured the dogs would spring up joyously, wag their tails, race across the ring, leap into their owners' arms, and plaster them with kisses. That's what my pugs do whenever I return home from a five-minute absence—at least the spring-up-joyously, tail-wagging parts. The obedience dogs, however, just lay there inert, while their owners, looking equally inert, stood beside them facing in the same direction until the judge signaled the end of the exercise.

Ironically, I was impressed. I say "ironically," and I say it in the proper sense of the word, because I'm normally as fond of regimentation as I am of liverwurst casserole with overcooked broccoli on the side. Yet for some reason—my dictatorial mindset, perhaps—I wanted to try this at home.

The next day I lugged out the telephone directory and looked up "Wonderdog Schools" in the Yellow Pages. There were no listings. I looked under "You Won't _____ing Believe This." Still no luck. Finally, by process of elimination, I arrived at "Dog Training" and selected the name of the canine finishing school nearest me.

A pleasant-sounding woman answered the phone. I had told her my name and had gotten as far as "I'm calling because…" when her voice was drowned out by cacophonous baying that sounded as if the hounds of hell were hot on the scent of a fox.

"SHUT UP!!!" the woman screamed.

I immediately broke off in midsentence. So did her dogs.

"[Shoot]," I thought, "this woman's good. I usually have to scream 'SHUT UP' three or four times before my dogs quiet down."

"She's not that good," my Alter Ego #1 chimed in. "She's just got a deeper voice than you have."

"Sorry about that," the trainer lady barked. "Go on."

I explained that I wanted to enroll one of my pugs, a male named Hans who was nearly two years old, in obedience training. The woman told me there wouldn't be another class for beginners until mid-February (nearly three months away). I had hoped to

Hans' jolly nature is belied by an expression that always looks as if he was just the recipient of bad news.

begin molding Hans into the perfect dog before then because he desperately needed molding, but as he would still be young enough to learn new tricks by the time February arrived, I signed him up for the eight-week beginner's course.

On a harsh February evening Hans and I arrived at the trainer's cold comfort farmette. Hans was tricked out in the expensive rolled leather collar and matching lead I had bought for him. (A "lead" is what civilians refer to as a "leash.") When I stepped inside the frigid "training centre," which looked as if it had been a tractor barn in a former life, I wished I had also bought Hans a sweater.

As I was walking in place trying to keep warm, the door to the training centre burst open and in raced a large German shepherd-Cujo mix. A split second later in flew a woman who was attached to the dog by a lead. Her hair was streaming out behind her, and her legs were churning so fast in an effort to keep from tripping and having her face exfoliated by the cold cement floor that she looked like a cartoon character.

"This is rich," I thought. "I wonder if that dog's going to stop in time when he notices the wall."

The dog put on the brakes and slid to a stop inches from the wall. The woman, meanwhile, had let go of the lead and had managed not to run up her dog's back. She picked up the lead quickly and gave a mighty tug to prevent her dog from trying to run her into another wall.

The main thing Hans learned that night was how to avoid the shepherd-Cujo's teeth, which made a serious pass at the throat of every dog that came within reach. Undaunted, Hans and I turned up again the following week. Eventually, by dint of grade inflation and considerable practice at home, Hans was awarded a diploma from the training academy at the end of eight weeks. By that time he was able—and generally willing—to walk beside me calmly on a lead, sit promptly when I stopped walking, remain sitting while I walked ten paces away then turned and faced him, and not budge until I called him, at which time he raced to where I stood and sat smartly in front of me. (Well, he raced just about all the time and sat smartly most of the time.) He had even begun to grasp the rudiments of the "down" command, the prelude to the "long down," which was the exercise I'd witnessed at the dog show several months before.

I'd like to say that Hans' progress in obedience school made him a better dog at home, but I can't. A dog's success in obedience—like a teenager's knack for geometry—does not always translate into civilized behavior outside the classroom. I know because I used to be pretty good at geometry. Consequently, no matter how often or how sharply I yelled "heel" or "sit" or "cut it the hell out," Hans persisted in launching himself into the air and crashing against the kitchen door at precisely the same time my wife was on the other side of door trying to open it.

Nor was the sit-stay exercise that Hans performed at the training centre of any use in keeping him quiet in the kitchen whenever someone rang the door bell. Like Pavlov's celebrated dog, Hans reacted promptly to the bell; instead of salivating, however, Hans barked at the top of his lungs while bouncing off the door separating the kitchen from the living room. I could have yelled "sit" until the person at the door retreated in fear, but Hans would have kept right on barking and bouncing. Thus, I had to resort to my former method of preventing Hans and our other pugs from racing into the living room and attacking the front door. That method involved serious yelling and a sweeping motion made with my right foot as I carefully opened the kitchen-living room door. Every time I

There were seven other dogs and their owners in the class, and I knew as soon as we entered the gymnasium that mid-October night that I was in serious company.

did, I imagined the dogs I had seen in the obedience class at the dog show sitting primly in their kitchens while their owners walked gracefully to the front door to welcome their visitors.

Thinking that perhaps Hans needed more training, I joined an obedience club that met during warm weather in a park about forty-five minutes from my house. The dogs in the intermediate class, to which Hans had been assigned, appeared to be well trained. I feared that Hans was in over his stubborn head, yet my house-devil turned street-angel in their company, picking up new instruction swiftly and placing fourth in the end-of-summer obedience match. He might have won if he hadn't decided to lie down during the "sit-stay" portion of the program, but that's Hans. He knew the "down-stay" was next, and he was probably in a hurry to get home as it was beginning to get dark. He's always tried to keep a step or two ahead of me, and he's usually been successful.

Hans' progress—and my persistent hope that he would some day become more docile at home—inspired me to enroll him in another training class that fall. This one was taught by a big-name trainer who had written a book or two about training and who charged accordingly for her services. There were seven other dogs and their owners in the class, and I knew as soon as we entered the gymnasium that mid-October night that I was in serious company. The other members of the class—all women—were either studiously obese (and looking to get control over something in their lives) or damn near anorexic (and determined to extend their control to their dogs' appetites as well as their own).

The dogs, who ran to Border collies and Welsh corgis, looked down their noses at the jolly Hans, who doesn't have enough nose to look down on anything except his food bowl. Nevertheless, he handled himself well during the first two sessions, and I began to hope that maybe this school would reveal the magic link between obedience in a controlled setting and obedience in our house.

My hopes were dashed forever in week three when we began working on an exercise called front-and-finish. In this routine the handler commands his or her dog to sit, marches ten paces in a fair approximation of a goose step, then turns and stands in a rigid military posture facing the dog. When the trainer says, "Call your dog," the handler says the dog's name, followed by the word "come." At that the dog bustles right up to the handler, sits down, and at a signal from its handler circles to the handler's right, reappears at the handler's left side, and sits down neatly, facing in the same direction as the handler.

When it came Hans' turn to perform this feat, which we had practiced many times—some more successfully than others—at home, I called Hans' name cheerfully. Hans cheerfully refused to budge. A few seconds passed. I felt my face getting red. A few more seconds passed. I began to sweat. Finally I walked to where Hans sat, took him by his collar, and began walking him slowly to the place from which I had called him. This, I thought, was in keeping with training protocol, which mandates that you never repeat a command. Instead you show the dog what you wanted him to do.

As I was towing Hans to the spot from which I had called him, the trainer said, "Just a minute."

I stopped.

"What would you do if he had disobeyed you at home?" she asked.

"I'd do what I'm doing now," I replied, as if I was answering a stupid question.

"You've got to show more authority," the trainer said. "Don't coax him. *Take* him to the spot where you want him to go—as if you mean business."

After I had walked Hans through the rest of the exercise, the trainer asked for another volunteer. A nervous-looking woman offered to demonstrate the exercise with her Border collie. All went well until the woman commanded the dog to quit his sitting position and run to her. The dog was running

Then I realized the cluckheads were clucking because the dog wasn't obeying promptly.

along happily until she got to a spot about five feet in front of the woman. The dog then slowed to a cower and fairly crawled with her tail between her legs until she was roughly two feet in front of her mistress.

A general clucking and tsk-tsking arose from the audience. At first I thought my fellow classmates were upset because the dog was obviously scared to death of what usually happened next. Then I realized the cluckheads were clucking because the dog wasn't obeying promptly.

The trainer told the lady to try the exercise again. Again the dog raced to a spot five feet in front of her owner and began crawling.

"Wow," I thought, "this lady must put a severe hurtin' on the dog if it doesn't finish the rest of the exercise."

Following more tsking and clucking from the peanut gallery, the trainer offered to work with the dog, but the dog wasn't inclined to get too close to her either. The trainer, looking chagrined, strode to the room she used for an office and reemerged with a long length of tow rope that looked strong enough to haul the Love Boat, fully loaded, into port.

The trainer proceeded to affix the rope to the poor dog's collar, then carefully laid forty feet or so of rope in a straight line. She then instructed the dog's owner to begin the exercise again.

The owner commanded the dog to stay, marched off ten paces, then turned to face the dog, one foot on either side of the rope. When the owner called the dog, she leaped up and ran toward her owner. All the while the trainer, who had taken a position twenty feet behind the owner, reeled in the rope as the dog ran. When the dog began to cower as she approached her owner, the trainer gave a Herculean yank on the rope, nearly lifting the dog off her feet and depositing her in front of her owner.

The members of the peanut gallery, save Hans and I, mumbled approvingly. I tried to look sternly disapproving while Hans tried to look small. Imagine our surprise, therefore, when the trainer asked me to try the front-and-finish exercise one more time with Hans. I looked down at the little guy, who looked back at me quizzically.

"With or without the rope?" I asked.

"Without," said the trainer.

I commanded Hans to sit, stepped off ten paces, turned to face him, and awaited further instruction. At a word from the trainer, I called Hans. This time he leaped up and raced toward me eagerly, looking focused and in command. I pictured him stopping in front of me, then executing a perfect finish.

While I was occupied with this vision, Hans veered slightly to my left and ran straight by me. He didn't stop running until he had reached the door of the gymnasium, where he sat expectantly as if waiting to be let out.

"It's the rope for you, partner," I said quietly as I carried Hans back to the classroom area. He knew I was kidding, as he probably knew I would ask that he be excused from the rest of the evening's festivities. He also knew, I'm sure, that he'd never see that woman or her tow rope again.

Chapter 10

Pug Olympics

The Games of the XXVIII Olympiad in August 2004 mark the third occasion that Athens has hosted the Olympics. Athens also hosted the Olympics in 1896, the year the Nobel Prizes and the state of Utah were established; and in 776 BCE, the year agoraphobia was invented.

Agoraphobia is commonly defined as the fear of open spaces, but originally it meant "fear of the *agora* (marketplace)." During the build up to the Games, we experience the symptoms of agoraphobia in the classic sense as the marketing offensive for the Olympics grows toward health-epidemic proportions. Buffeted by the Official Theme Music of the Olympic Games in supermarkets and shopping malls, assaulted by pop-up ads for the Official Hemorrhoid Cream of the Olympic Games on every other Web site, pepper-sprayed by fifteen-second Olympic Memories on television, and driven to despair when both major-party presidential hopefuls begin referring to themselves as the Official Candidate of the Olympic Games, Americans desperate for relief create a huge demand for bootlegged copies of *Pluto Nash*, *Joe Dirt*, and Wyclef Jean's sampling of "The Complete Speeches of Gerald Ford."

Before people's minds turn to gumbo from encountering yet another exclusive interview with the hair stylist for the United States synchronized-swimming team or the astrologist who counsels the rhythmic gymnasts, I would like to announce the opening of the campaign to have pugs declared the Official Dogs of the Olympic Games.

This campaign does not seek a mere bought-and-paid-for commercial honor such as the commission of Stim-U-Dent® as the Official Plaque Remover of the Olympic Games. I am suggesting that pugs boldly go where no other breed has yet to tread—into the Olympic locker room and arena as full-fledged participants in the games. Pugs deserve elevation to Olympic status in recognition of their athletic achievements. Indeed, three games at which pugs have traditionally excelled are worthy of inclusion in the 2008 Olympics, which will be held in Beijing, China—the country where pug dogs originated. The Official Pug Olympic Games are Barking at Equines, Human Tripping, and Window Fogging.

Before I describe the rules for these games and the world-record achievements in each, I must take a moment to urge you to write the International Olympic Committee and suggest that pug sports be added to the 2008 Olympic roster. If three-legged shuffleboard, underwater bowling, and other "sports" that people play only once every four years are deserving of Olympic status, then Barking at Equines, Human Tripping, and Window Fogging surely merit a place on the schedule. I should also remind you that it is acceptable to send cash in large denominations when writing to any member of the International Olympic Committee.

Barking at Equines

Any horse, mule, jackass, or donkey (I never knew the difference among the last three) is an appropriate target for Barking at Equines. The playing field for this contest comprises sixteen Olympic-sized pastures arranged in a four-by-four grid and separated by two-lane roads. An Olympic-sized pasture is eight hectares (twenty acres). Five equines are placed in each of four pastures. No pasture containing equines may be bordered by another pasture containing them. The cost of preparing this field and housing the equines is modest compared to the cost of removing three thousand television antennae from rooftops in Athens and replacing them with underground cable in order to provide a more aesthetic aerial view of the marathon and other Olympic events. What's more, no animals will be harmed during the competition.

After the equines have been deployed, four pug athletes are placed in a 2008 Dodge Caravan, the Official Minivan of the Olympic Games. The pugs are then driven at a speed between 56.3 and 64.4 kilometers per hour (35 to 40 mph) along the roads separating the pastures.

Three points are awarded to the first pug to bark after spotting an equine. At that point, the driver stops the van for ninety seconds to allow the contestants sufficient barking time. Two bonus points are awarded if the pug that barked first is still barking after ninety seconds have elapsed. The driver then proceeds to the next pasture containing equines.

One point is deducted if a dog barks at the pictures of Lassie on billboards that have been placed in three of the empty pastures. Barking at Lassie automatically results in a ninety-second timeout so that all competitors have a chance to stop barking and compose themselves.

A competitor is disqualified if he or she attacks another competitor during the match, thereby causing that competitor to bark at the attacker instead of an equine. Competitors are also disqualified for soiling the van. The winners of each round of Barking at Equines compete in subsequent rounds until the Olympic champion is determined.

The unofficial world record holder in Barking at Equines is a fawn pug named Debby, who was four years old when she scored a thirteen on April 29, 1995. Debby's score is unofficial because it was recorded along a stretch of highway just outside of Intercourse, Pennsylvania, instead of an Olympic course.

Debby scored three points for being the first pug in the van to spot a horse and begin barking on three different occasions, and four points for barking damn near half the thirty-mile ride home. (Debby, who was a legendary barker, also recorded the highest score in the unofficial sport of indoor barking at equines when she barked nonstop for more than twenty minutes during the broadcast of the 1996 Kentucky Derby.)

Human Tripping

As its name implies, Human Tripping is an event in which the pug athlete attempts to trip a human by stepping or lying in front of or behind that person. After each pug athlete in Human Tripping has drawn a human "target," that target begins preparing a traditional Greek salad and a gyro in an Official Olympic Kitchen using products supplied by General Electric, the Official Electricity of the Olympic Games. All human targets must be roughly the same size, weight, and age, and must possess twenty-twenty vision. Meal preparation must last at least thirty minutes, and no points will be awarded beyond that limit.

Two points are awarded for making targets look stupid and ungainly as they flail their arms and try to keep their balance after being tripped. Four points go to the pug that causes a target to drop something while stumbling and looking stupid, five points if that object breaks, six points if it is edible and the pug begins to lick or bite it before the target can intervene. One point is deducted if a dropped object or a spilled substance falls on the pug.

Unlike the "sport" of Horse Tripping, which has been banned at all events sanctioned by the Professional Rodeo Cowboys Association, the contestants in Human Tripping are not rewarded for "downing" their targets. In fact, two points are deducted if the target is downed (both knees must be touching the floor for at least one second at the same time in order for an target to be considered down). Three such knockdowns within thirty minutes are cause for disqualification. A pug can also be disqualified if a downed target is injured badly enough to prevent him or her from completing at least thirty minutes of meal preparation.

The current world record holder in Human Tripping is Ella, a fawn girl who was not yet two when she amassed twenty points on January 16, 1994. Ella caused the author to stumble on five occasions during that memorable performance (ten points). She also caused him to drop and break a salad bowl (five points) and to drop a red bell pepper, which she promptly began chewing (six points).

One point was deducted from her score when Ella failed to get out of the way of a salad shooter the author had dropped.

Window Fogging

A team sport played with five pugs on a side, Window Fogging involves snorting, sneezing, spraying, and spewing upper respiratory fluids on the windows of a Dodge Caravan, the Official Minivan of the Olympic Games, during a one-hour ride in the downtown area of the host city of the games. Five points are awarded for partially obstructing any passenger window; ten points if the window is rendered completely opaque. Bonus points are added, two points per inch or portion thereof, for length of upper-respiratory-fluid drip. (Said drip must be at least one-eighth of an inch wide in order to qualify.)

The current world record holder for Window Fogging is the team of Percy, Debby, Patty (captain), Ella, and Hans. On July 16, 1994, this team earned the splendid total of sixty-two points by completely obscuring five side windows in a Dodge Caravan (fifty points). Several small rivulets of varying lengths contributed twelve additional points to this record score.

On Sunday, August 29, 2004, the FedEx® Olympic torch will be extinguished by Muhammad Ali as a choir of five hundred Cher impersonators, conducted by Rudolph Giuliani, the Official Ex-Mayor of the Olympic Games, sings "Freedom" by Paul McCartney, the Official Ex-Beatle of the Olympic Games. By then roughly 10,500 athletes will have competed for 301 gold medals in thirty-seven sports. The contests will have been viewed by 4.2 million spectators and 21,600 members of the media.

The absence of pugs from these contests would, of course, be an oversight of Olympic proportion. Pug lovers must not allow this oversight to occur. Thus, before you queue up for that copy of *Pluto Nash*, please take a minute to remind the members of the International Olympic Committee that the skill, grace, and dedication of pug athletes are an inspiration to performers of all races, creeds, sexual preferences, and species. And remember: when you send cash to an Olympic official through the mail, it is best not to put your return address on the envelope.

June and Skippy the Cat resting near a print of Saint Pugnacious, whose likeness suddenly appeared on a towel with which he had been dried.

Chapter 11

Is Your Pug Bow-Lingual?

Half an hour before her dinner time, your pug begins to bark. She is barking because: a) there's a serial killer at your front door dressed as an Avon Lady; b) a surveillance helicopter is about to crash through the kitchen window; c) the pheasant breast *en croûte* just burst into flames in the oven; d) she's hungry.

You grab your car keys from the rack in the kitchen and head for the door. Your pug begins to bark. He is barking because: a) you're not wearing shoes; b) he's not wearing shoes; c) an eel just crawled out of your sink; d) he wants to go with you.

It's five o'clock in the morning and you're in the middle of the most meaningful dream you've ever had. Your pugs begin to bark. They are barking because: a) that's not your significant other in the dream; b) you have just wet the bed; c) the cat's chewing on the cord of your electric blanket; d) they have to pee.

If you had trouble answering any of these questions without moving your lips, a Japanese toy maker has the answer to your problem(s). The toy maker is Takara; the answer is Bow-Lingual™, a devilish gadget that translates dog barks into human language.

Available in pet stores, gift shops, and other retail outlets, Bow-Lingual consists of a three-inch-long wireless microphone and a fits-in-your-palm console about the size of a credit card. If you're wondering why your pug begins to bark every day about half an hour before dinner time, Bow-Lingual will ease your mind for a mere $120 (American).

To operate Bow-Lingual, just hitch the microphone to Pugsley's collar. When he begins to bark, the microphone will transmit that bark to the console, which will compare his bark to a large sample of other canine utterances stored in a self-contained database. Quicker than you can say, "I wonder what he means by that?" Bow-Lingual will classify your dog's bark into one of six emotional categories: happiness, sadness, frustration, anger, assertion, or desire. The console's liquid-crystal display will then exhibit a message that corresponds to Pugsley's emotional state. At that point you can begin fixing Pugsley's dinner, secure in the knowledge that he was barking because he was hungry and not because he was trying to remind you that there's a rerun of *Milo and Otis* on the Bravo channel tonight at eight o'clock.

In addition to sending you text messages from your dog, Bow-Lingual contains a data analyzer that can diagnose a dog's happiness level, determine her friendliness toward other dogs, and compile a diary of a dog's feelings during a specified period of time. If the chewed-up woodwork in the kitchen doesn't tell you that your dog is bored, you can always check his diary to be sure. After all, he might be trying to say he needs more fiber in his diet.

Bow-Lingual was developed by the Japan Acoustic Laboratory and a Japanese cellphone-content provider called Index Corporation. During three year's research using voiceprint-analysis technology, scientists gathered and stored two thousand digital vocal patterns from one thousand dogs of more than fifty breeds, from German shepherds to Chihuahuas. These vocal patterns were then analyzed by a panel of animal behavior experts and pet owners, who sorted the patterns into the aforementioned six emotional categories: happiness, sadness, frustration, anger, assertion, or desire.

If you ask me—and even if you don't—the makers of Bow-Lingual are barking up the wrong tree. Nobody with the sense not to gaze upward during a rainstorm needs a canine mood ring to tell him why a pug is barking. Furthermore, pugs display a richer emotional tapestry than the six moods featured on Bow-Lingual. What about the pug's sense of irony? Or whimsey? Or stoic resignation? I have also detected at times a sense of existential longing, not to

Patty excels at shelling walnuts and at playing soccer with them.

mention agnosticism, in my dogs. Where are the words to express such deeply felt modes of being?

Finally, pugs have a more creative vocabulary than that contained in the Bow-Lingual responses I've seen quoted in the press, most of which sound like English subtitles for Japanese monster movies. If a pug were experiencing anger, for example, she wouldn't say, "You're ticking me off," as Bow-Lingual alleges she would. Our pugs would be more likely to say, "Listen, toilet breath, you're really starting to fry my ass."

Nevertheless, one Takara executive cites phrasing as the key to Bow-Lingual's success in Japan, where, according to news reports, sales exceeded 300,000 units during the gadget's first year on the market. "If we translated sad emotions just as 'I'm sad,' it wouldn't be interesting at all," said the executive. Instead such feelings are expressed as "Have you forgotten about me?" or "I'm blue and I want to cry."

"I'm blue and I want to cry"! Any pug who would say that has been listening to too much elevator jazz.

Despite Bow-Lingual's howling shortcomings, *Time* magazine, a perennial bastion of alt.culture hipness, included Bow-Lingual among the coolest inventions of 2002, along with a phone tooth and a Braille glove that translates hand signs into speech. Come to think of it, the former does have promising applications. You could plant one in your dog then call him up when it's time for him to come in from the yard. The talking tooth could also revolutionize obedience competition. As for the Braille glove, I could put my finger on at least one creative use for that gizmo.

Takara, meanwhile, is planning a cell phone modification that will enable Bow-Lingual to be read on mobile phones. I am already on record as being firmly against dogs having cell phones (see Chapter 16, page 92), so I will not comment on the absurdity of that idea.

At this stage of development, the only thing that might save America from Bow-Lingual is the fear of litigation. What happens, for example, if a child playing with Bow-Lingual is bitten by a dog who just said to him, "Let's play. I like your sailor suit"?

Whom do you sue? Was the dog lying? Did Bow-Lingual lose something in translation? Is the dog's owner responsible? Katsuhisa Oda, a spokesman for the Index Corporation, is justifiably worried about liability issues in the United States, the land where a burglar who accidentally locked himself in the garage of a house he was robbing sued the owners of the house for pain and suffering—and won—because he was stuck in the garage for four days without anything to eat while the owners were away on vacation.

As lame as Bow-Lingual rates as an interspecies communicator, it could make a great party toy for humans. Get half a dozen folks and a case of beer. Have one person bark into the microphone and another person act out Bow-Lingual's translation of the bark. That could be interesting, especially when Bow-Lingual interprets a bark as signifying desire.

Chapter 12
Why Air Isn't Free

On a dank-gray Monday morning as I was waiting for my muse to show up for work, I received a phone call from Don, the mechanic at the Garrettown Garage, where I had left my beloved 1993 Dodge Caravan for servicing an hour earlier. (With the exception of the make and model of the van, the names in this account have been changed to protect me.)

I had taken the van to the garage to have a new evaporator installed. An evaporator, for the mechanically impaired, is a gizmo that helps to prevent cream cheese from forming in automobile air conditioners. When the evaporator goes south, there's a critical increase in the temperature inside the vehicle, accompanied by a lethal odor that smells worse than a landfill on a hot August day.

Don the mechanic was calling to inquire if I was the person who had dropped off the gray Dodge Caravan that morning. There couldn't have been more censure in his tone had he asked if he were speaking to the prime suspect in the JonBenet Ramsey murder investigation. When I replied that I was the owner of the van, Don informed me he couldn't work on it "because of all that dog hair."

"Say again?" I thought. "Too much dog hair? Is this guy the Niles Crane of the Snap-on™ set? Where does he think he's working, Martha Stewart's garage?"

In my mind's eye, which normally runs about twenty-sixty, I had a vision of Don returning home from work in his mechanic's suit, looking as if he'd been swimming in a major oil spill. He's about to sit down with *The Wall Street Journal* when his wife rushes into the library and screams, "Change you clothes. I don't want you getting dog hair all over that Eames chair."

"Huh?" I finally said. It was the only thing I could think to say, which was rather an embarrassment for somebody in the communication racket.

"You'll have to take the van somewhere and get it cleaned before I'll work on it," said Don. "There's too much dog hair."

Thinking nimbly, I told Don that I failed to see how dog hair in the van would prevent him from working on the air conditioner. I was tempted to point out that there wasn't too much dog hair in the van because it hadn't drifted higher than the seats, but he was probably using that damn metric system.

"I have to lie on the floor in front of the seats to take the dashboard out to work on the air conditioner," said Don, "and there's just too much dog hair in there."

I was speechless. Stone mute. "Does this guy wear a white linen suit to work between Memorial Day and Labor Day?" I thought. Then my mind went catatonic with the embarrassment of it all. The Garrettown Garage, where Don is employed, isn't one of those gleaming operations where the service manager dresses like a maître d' and the technicians sport Gucci work shoes and flawless manicures. This garage, which also sells the odd new car, looks as if it's on loan from a Norman Rockwell painting. There are people in the greater Garrettown area who have more cars in their front yards than this garage has on its lot. The showroom, which has a wooden floor and is no bigger than my living room, has one dusty car in it. In lieu of a Rolodex, there are a bunch of telephone numbers scribbled on a blotter near the rotary phone. I have been denied service in shabbier places, but not when I was sober.

"What if he reports me to the Pennsylvania Bureau of Upholstery and Car Rugs?" I thought. "What if he runs his mouth over at Bubba's Beer and Barbeque on wet T-shirt night?" I feared that whenever I went to Cuzzin's Country Market, people would take the plastic rod that's supposed to keep their groceries from fraternizing with other customers' groceries and place it on the floor behind them so they wouldn't have to fraternize with me.

Although puppies enjoy playing with Uncle Hans, they frequently complain about his changing the rules in midgame.

After communication between my brain and vocal cords finally had been restored, I said to Don, "This is incredible. I'm [age withheld at the author's request], and I've owned cars since I was sixteen years old. You're the first mechanic I've ever met who was too delicate to work on one."

"I'm not delicate," said Don, lowering his voice an octave for effect, "but I'm not working in all that dog hair."

"Fine," I said. "I hope you know somebody who needs an evaporator."

"I'm sure we can sell it," he replied.

I relate all this not only because I'm writing a book but also because I feel it's my civic duty. Unless pug owners start vacuuming their vehicles before taking them in for service, garages will begin imposing a dog-hair tax on all vehicles. I am unanimous about this because I speak from experience.

I'm not proud to admit it, but I'm the guy responsible for the fact that air is no longer free at many garages. I was going to mention this at the beginning of this chapter, but I was afraid of losing too many readers.

Twenty-three years ago I pulled into a Texaco station in West Chester, Pennsylvania, to put air in the chronically low right front tire of the car I was driving. (Besides never asking for directions, guys would sooner keep putting air in tires than get them repaired.) Air, like the American people, was free in those days, so I was startled to hear a voice say "I ought to charge people like you for air" as I was topping up my tire.

"What?" I said.

"I don't like your bumper sticker," replied the voice, which belonged to a young man who was standing in the doorway of the gas station office glaring at me.

"But it's true," I protested, nodding toward the bumper sticker. "More people *have* died in Ted Kennedy's car than in nuclear power plants."

"I don't care," said the voice. "The next time you come around there's going to be a sign on that pump that says 'Air 25 Cents.'"

Chapter 13

Getting My Goat

A team of scientists, spiders, and West African goats holed up on a converted maple-sugar farm in a remote section of Quebec is working to save lives—and to corner the market on biodegradable fishing line. Toward those ends, this diligent crew has collaborated to forge BioSteel®. Five times stronger than ordinary steel, this marvel of genetic engineering is hardy enough to turn back a speeding bullet, yet sheer enough to rest lightly on the stiletto shoulders of the most anorexic fashion model—no small consideration if she ever finds herself in need of a bullet-proof bustier.

History does not record whose round it was when somebody in a wrinkled lab coat jumped up and said, "I've got an idea. Let's take the silk-spinning gene from a golden orb-weaving spider and stick that sucker into a goat egg; but before we put the spider gene into the goat egg, we'll rig the gene so that it works only in the mammary gland when a she-goat produces milk. After that we figure out how to separate the silk from the milk, then we corner the market on bio-degradable fishing line."

The company formed to hitch its profit margin to this brain-storm is called Nexia Biotechnologies (www.nexiabiotech.com), whose headquarters are fifteen miles from the aforementioned farm in Quebec. According to the June 16, 2002 *New York Times*, Nexia researchers not only perfected the sleight-of-gland gene transfer but also figured out how to separate the resultant silk from the goats' milk. Consequently, the *Times* reported, "Nexia foresees tapping into the $500 million market for fishing materials as well as the $1.6 billion market for industrial fibers in the near future.

"The haute-couture world is already intrigued by a nearly weightless gossamer-like fabric," the *Times* continued; but the prime booty call came from the Pentagon, "which is working with Nexia to develop a [bulletproof] vest that might be made entirely out of goat silk."

In addition to fishing lines and vests, BioSteel may also be used to make artificial ligaments, medical sutures, and coatings for space stations. One further suspects that goat silk would make high-fashion, bulletproof thongs or nonshredding dental floss.

The resultant transgenic pugs, should they ever lock their owners out of the car, would be able to open the door.

"That's cool," you say, "but what has all this got to do with pug dogs?"

I'm glad you asked. Recently I incorporated Lock, Stuck, and Batter, a biotech research foundation, and I am seeking research proposals and donations of large sums of money so that I can assemble a team of scientists to work on a similar gene-splicing experiment involving pugs.

Scientists employed by Lock, Stuck, and Batter, whose corporate headquarters are located in a laptop computer in southeastern Pennsylvania, will seek to extract genetic material from human locksmiths and to splice that material into pug dog eggs. The resultant transgenic pugs, should they ever lock their owners out of the car, would be able to open the door. Before inserting the locksmith genes into the pug eggs, however, the Lock, Stuck, and Batter scientists will deactivate the genes governing the following locksmith behaviors: a) informing callers that there will be at least a forty-five minute wait and b) announcing that there's an extra charge for service on weekends.

I first recognized the need for Lock, Stuck, and Batter on a hot Sunday afternoon in August 1998, after I had visited a bookstore about twenty-five miles from my house to pick up the Andrew Wyeth biography that had been published earlier that year. From the bookstore, I proceeded to one of my favorite Italian restaurants for some quiet reading and an al dente meal. I was escorted by an

Burt (left) and Fetch trying to convince the lady at the take-out window to add a couple of Whoppers to the order.

honor guard of five pugs: the sacred girl-dog June; her two sons, Burt and Harry; their bachelor uncle Hans; and his aunt Ella.

I pulled up across from the restaurant, parked the van in a spot I would be able to monitor from a window table inside the restaurant, checked to see that the air conditioner was set to "arctic," then took my spare set of keys and my book and got out of the van. I left the motor running and the air conditioner on so the dogs would be comfortable while I was in the restaurant.

Something in that exiting-the-van sequence must have wakened Ella, and something in her brain must have told her we were home, because she waddled across the front floor of the van, poured herself out the door before I could close it, and shuffled off in search of her yard.

I tossed my spare keys and book onto the seat, closed the door, and began pursuing Ella, who crouched down with her tail between her legs as though this were the part where I beat her about the head and neck. As I moved toward her slowly, I could hear the other dogs

> *There I was, locked out of the van with nineteen pounds of limp pug under my arm and a hot, unforgiving sun smirking down.*

in the van cheering her on. They sounded like convicts in a prison yard when a fight breaks out.

Fortunately, Ella soon realized she was not in her driveway, at which point she began to look worried and waited for me to pick her up. Unfortunately, one member of the chorus that was cheering her on had mashed down the lock on the inside of the driver's side door. There I was, locked out of the van with nineteen pounds of limp pug under my arm and a hot, unforgiving sun smirking down.

As I was glaring and cursing silently at the dogs in the van, who were dancing up and down and thumbing their noses at me, a gentleman came along and said he had witnessed the entire scene. He wanted to know if there was anything he could do to help. I asked him if he had a gun. He didn't, so we walked over to his car and consulted his trunk. I noticed with some embarrassment that *his* car windows weren't covered with dog snot; *his* cargo space wasn't carpeted with dog hair; and *he* wasn't standing there with a sagging pug under his arm feeling sorry for himself. I was about to point this out to Ella, but she had fallen asleep.

After we had retrieved the gentleman's tire iron, which wasn't even pointy at one end the way a decent tire iron is supposed to be, we feared there wasn't any way we could use it to pry open a window of the van. We were right, but in the attempt we discovered that the passenger-side window hadn't been rolled up to the hilt. Thus, we were able to coax it down three-quarters of an inch or so, just far enough to insert another disgustingly clean tool from the gentleman's trunk—a long rod with a couple of ninety-degree angles in it and a hook at one end. It looked like the kind of thing a gastroenterologist might carry around. I watched as he carefully inserted the strange-looking instrument into the space above the passenger side window. Alas, the hook reached only to the top of the lock.

My wife was away for the afternoon—with only one dog, I might add—so there was no point in calling home; and the cops, whom the gentleman's wife had called on a cell phone, said they weren't allowed to break into people's vehicles—at least not when there were other people around. Next we tried a locksmith, who said he wouldn't be able to get to us for at least forty-five minutes and there was an extra charge for service on weekends.

I feared that Ella, who was now wide aware and panting heavily, would be toast if she had to spend forty-five minutes outdoors in ninety-some-degree weather, so there was nothing to do but smash a window. I didn't think it would be difficult. Not that long ago we'd had to replace a windshield in the van after it had been cracked by a "rock" no bigger than a tooth filling.

Warning everyone to stand back and handing Ella to the gentleman with the surgically clean car—"at least we can get some dog hair on his clothes," I snickered to myself—I gave the window of the sliding cargo door a vigorous thump.

Give people enough superstrength fishing line and they'll try to hang you with it.

That quieted the dogs in the van momentarily, but it made no impression on the window. Nor did the three or four additional whacks I gave the glass.

Just as I was about to ask the gentleman, who was still holding Ella, what he would give me for her, the van, and its contents (excluding the new, richly illustrated Wyeth biography), a woman driving past stopped to ask whether we could use a coat hanger. I assured her that we could, and before long the antiseptically clean gentleman who had come to my aid used the coat hanger to fish open the passenger-side door of the van. I thanked him profusely, took Ella from his arms, and placed her carefully on the van seat. I gathered up my spare keys and my new book, locked the van, and headed for the restaurant.

When the initial public offering of Lock, Stuck, and Batter stock becomes available, I am sure the response will be enthusiastic. Some cynics may sniff that Lock, Stuck, and Batter's research can't hold a firearm to Nexia Biotechnologies' quest for a space-age fishing line or bulletproof thongs. That's the way of the world. Give people enough superstrength fishing line and they'll try to hang you with it. I would merely remind those cynics that pug owners who take their dogs for rides in the car are going to get locked out far more often than they're going to get shot in the chest.

Chapter 14
Pug Haiku

Haiku (high-*koo*), as many people know, is a bite-sized form of Japanese poetry invented four centuries ago by Zen monks with attention deficit disorder (ADD). What people may not know, however, is the extent of haiku's popularity. If you're thinking that haiku is no more ubiquitous than sushi bars on the Left Coast or kudzu in the Southeast, you've got another nori roll coming. Anyone who wants to read a book of haiku would have nearly five hundred titles from which to choose—everything from *Cold Moon: The Erotic Haiku of Gabriel Rosenstock* (for those in the mood for a quickie) to *Haikus for Jews: For You, a Little Wisdom* (gefilte fish for the soul). People looking for haiku online have 1.3 million Web sites to peruse, including examples of dog haiku at www.yuckles.com/doghaikus.htm.

If you're beginning to wonder why haiku is so popular, you're not alone. I've been wondering the same thing myself. Coincidentally, I was wondering this just as I was starting to wonder what I was going to write about in this chapter. That's when I realized that I had never seen haiku about pug dogs. I vowed to correct that oversight at once, but before I reveal my plan for establishing the Multinational Institute for the Spawning of Haiku about Pugs (MISHAP), let us (re)consider the essentials of this art form.

Haiku, as I mentioned, was invented by Zen monks with ADD. Therefore, haiku consists of only seventeen syllables scattered across three lines; and, because people afflicted with ADD are notoriously bad at coming up with rhymes, haiku doesn't have any. It does, however, have one strict rule, which people often forget to observe:

the first and third lines in a haiku each contain five syllables, while the middle line has seven.

Some haiku authorities—the Matsuyama Municipal Shiki Memorial Museum, for example—contend that genuine haiku "takes nature in each season as its theme and expresses inspiration derived from nature." Thus, says the museum, every haiku should contain a "season word" like *summer, fall, winter, spring, football, hunting,* or *hay fever.* Yet this rule is violated so frequently that no one bothers to mention it any more except writers trying to fill up space in books.

As you might expect, freeing people of the restraints of having to color within the lines of rhyme and meter has a liberating effect on the Poetry Muse. Folks who might not feel up to expressing themselves in rhymed couplets of iambic pentameter don't seem at all reluctant about tossing off a haiku or ten when the inspiration strikes, no matter what the season. Moreover, people who would ordinarily hesitate about writing, say, an Elizabethan sonnet in the first-person-canine voice feel no such inhibition when it comes to haiku. As a consequence there is a small but comprehensive school of haiku written from a dog's point of view. To wit:

> *Today I have sniffed*
> *Many dog's butts—I celebrate*
> *By licking your face.*
>   Anonymous

This poem deftly illustrates the use of haiku to record the essence of a moment keenly perceived. Indeed, the author perceived the essence of this moment so keenly that he or she put eight syllables in the second line instead of seven, while simultaneously forgetting that the apostrophe goes outside the *s* in plural possessives. Yet such oversight is understandable. Who hasn't ignored the rules of grammar when overtaken by the essence of a moment?

Although no one knows who wrote the first canine haiku, for one glorious fortnight a few years ago, canine haiku appeared to be the fastest growing form of doggerel. This growth was documented by Cleveland's *Plain Dealer*, which reported that the response "was unbelievable" after a morning disc jockey on WNIR-FM in Akron, Ohio, had read some examples of canine haiku on the air. Afterward the station was dogged with requests for canine haiku and peppered with additional examples of the genre, such as:

> *I lie belly-up*
> *In the sunshine, happier than*
> *You ever will be.*
>
> Anonymous

Once again the second line contains eight syllables though it could just as easily have sported the requisite seven if the author had substituted *sun* for *sunshine*. What *is* this world coming to? Doesn't anybody proofread any more?

No sooner had canine haiku hit the airwaves than it bounced off into cyberspace. Yet even though there are several Web sites featuring canine haiku, the diligent student of literature will find the same eighteen to twenty poems on all those sites; and none of those poems, as I have noted, is by or about a pug dog.

If eighteen to twenty poems constitute the entire corpus of canine haiku, they are as so many fleas on the butt of the haiku world. The Spam haiku Web site (*http://pemtropics.mit.edu/~jcho/spam/*) packs a canned, searchable database that contains more than 17,800 haiku in praise of Spam. I was especially touched by SPAM-ku #17,839:

> *SPAM for midnight snack:*
> *Put can on plate and pressed START.*
> *Broken microwave.*
>
> —The Amazing Dan-San of the SPAM can

If Spam lovers can produce nearly eighteen thousand haiku, pug people ought to be able to come up with a few thousand of their own. There must be more than 100,000 pug owners around the world. If two percent of those owners took the time to write down seventeen syllables' worth of inspiration about their pugs, we'd have two thousand entries for MISHAP.

*Hans, on the lectern, poses with several members of the 1995 class of the
Elverson Pug Academy.*   *Photo by Jeff Keefe*

Those readers wondering who will assume the Lilliputian task
of maintaining such a repository need not worry. In the spirit of
public service (and a slight hangover), I humbly offer my services to
catalog pug haiku and my Web site (www.pugbus.com) to host
MISHAP. I invite all readers to join me in thinking big by thinking
small. Send your pug haiku to *phil@pugbus.com*. No poem will be
refused as long as it contains the word *pug*, either singular or plural,
or a word that contains the letters *p-u-g*, as in *pugnacious*.

Before you rush to your keyboard or quill, I should warn you
that you're dealing with a former school teacher here, so your haiku
better have five syllables in the first and third lines and seven syllables in the middle line, or your work will be rejected. If you want me
to include your name with your haiku when I post it, please say so.
To help goose the muse, I submit the following examples of pug
haiku:

#1

Our pugs' ransom note:
"We demand real food products
Not cheap by-products."

#2
How selfless the pug,
Who helps clean the litter box
Without our asking.

#3
"Why," thinks the puglet,
"Do humans make us practice
House-training outdoors?"

#4
Pugs must find us odd.
We run after buses, but
Scream if they chase cars.

#5
"Not another walk,"
The pug moans. "I hope she meets
A decent man soon."

#6
Pug ate my homework?
Nah. Who's going to believe
That lame old excuse?

#7
Pug strives to act couth,
But his behavior declares,
"I am a leg man."

#8
Wet, post-dinner kiss.
Essence of Kal-Kan. Oh how
Pugs leave me breathless.

#9
"So who needs e-mail?"
Asks the pug as he hikes a
Leg at the lamppost.

#10
Feeling pugnacious
And a trifle repugnant?
Kiss your pug instead.

Chapter 15
The Social Life of Pugs

Few sounds are more incongruous than the sound of pug dogs howling. A breed that couldn't survive in the wild without an ATM card and a ready source of take-out food, the pug has no more business howling than a slug has training for the hundred-meter dash. Therefore, when I heard bone-chilling howls emerge from the vicinity of our first-floor bedroom one afternoon, I assumed that a few hibernating members of the wolf packs last seen around these parts five thousand years ago had awakened hungry and, not realizing they had lost the property-rights wars to developers a long time since, were trying to scare up a meal.

I clutched a frying pan and tip-toed to the bedroom to investigate. Imagine my surprise when I discovered the source of the howling: the upraised heads of our youngest pugs, Burt and Harry, age one, who had awakened hungry and were obviously trying to scare up someone who might scare up a can opener. I laughed so hard I nearly dropped the frying pan.

Our other six pugs, all of them older than Burt and Harry, were lazing about the kitchen at the time, hoping as always that I might spill some of the food I was preparing. They didn't seem to be surprised or bothered by Burt's and Harry's outburst. "Oh," I could see them thinking, "don't those stupid dogs know that wolves lost the property-rights wars to developers a long time ago?"

I couldn't help but wonder at the sociological import of Burt's and Harry's performance. Were they practicing for the latest variation on the AKC's "sport" of showing dogs—a tandem karaoke tournament? Had they been possessed by some shape-shifting Cujo who would soon be feasting on our entrails? Had somebody slipped funny mushrooms into last night's stir fry that I was reheating?

What with all the pug "collectibles" we've acquired, The Graceland of Canine Company would be a more fitting description of our house.

Similar thoughts have continued to puzzle me since that landmark afternoon when Burt and Harry began to howl. What's more, my bafflement has grown as, one by one, our other pugs have begun to emulate the youngsters' behavior; and if there is nothing more incongruous than the sound of two pugs howling, it has to be the sound (and sight) of eight pugs convened in a quasi-circle, heads thrown back, throats extended, making a baleful noise in unison if not precisely in harmony.

No closer to an explanation for this behavior than I had been when I first heard it, I stumbled upon Elizabeth Marshall Thomas' book, *The Social Lives of Dogs*, in Borders one afternoon. The title led me to suspect that the answer to the howling pugs mystery pugs might be contained in this book, though I must admit I was put off by the subtitle: *The Grace of Canine Company*. What with all the pug "collectibles" we've acquired, *The Graceland of Canine Company* would be a more fitting description of our house. Nevertheless, I headed for the check-out line. I wish I could record the exact time of my seminal discovery, but Borders, obviously working on the theory that time flies when you're having fun, doesn't permit clocks in its local emporium.

The author of *The Social Lives of Dogs* is a trained anthropologist of a certain age who became famous for not altering her dogs, allowing them to reproduce and to run free at will, and then writing a best-selling book about it all entitled *The Hidden Life of Dogs*. I must admit I am not a trained anthropologist, but I am of a certain age—the "over-twenty-five group," my wife calls it—and I do spend a lot of time watching our dogs at play and at rest (largely at rest). Therefore, I felt I was at least marginally qualified to record my observations about the social lives of pug dogs and, more specifically, the reason(s) for our dogs' howling.

Even if I couldn't stretch my observations into a full-length best-selling book, I might get a book chapter out of them, for, as Thomas maintains, "…the life of a dog in an ordinary household can be fully as complex and instructive to observe as the life of a wild animal or a dog in an all-dog pack." To be sure, the lives of humans in similar households often resemble the lives of wild animals or of dogs in an all-dog pack, as anyone who has attempted to eat in the presence of more than two pugs knows only too well.

The first discovery I made after determining to study my dogs' behavior was that anthropological research, like real estate sales, turns largely on location. Therefore, the budding researcher must choose the site for his or her study wisely. To test your skills in this all-important area, consider the following: there are two kinds of anthropological investigations. The first demands your presence in some godforsaken backwater that doesn't provide high-speed Internet access and doesn't take American Express—a steaming jungle, for example, infested with six-pound mosquitos and flying snakes. The other kind of anthropological study occurs at home, where you don't have to endure any discomfort unless you're foolish enough to investigate the social lives of cats.

Which setting would you choose? Before declaring your final answer, ask yourself or someone near to you if your house is already the well-marked preserve of the pug colony you wish to study.

Like any anthropologist worth his or her Orvis clothes, I had to set up a proper observation site from which to record our dogs' social interactions. In fact, I set up three sites, all of which allowed me to jot down my observations without having to sleep in field, stream, or inclement weather. My primary on-site observation post was our east-facing bedroom window. I chose this site because it afforded me a fine place from which I could observe our dogs in the wild that used to be our yard. All I had to do was raise the Venetian blind, put a CD on, fetch a pen, notebook, and a snack, climb into my Orvis cargo pants, and pull up a chair at the window. Instant biosphere. My own focus group at play and at rest (largely at rest).

My secondary observation site—from which I could observe our pugs' indoor behavior by simply getting a pen, notebook, and a snack and slipping into my Orvis safari duds—was the kitchen table; and my third site, an excellent place for the nocturnal field work that no self-respecting anthropologist can ignore, was our bed, a king-sized affair that sleeps several pugs comfortably and two humans cautiously. There I could observe pugs in their den by getting a snack, putting on my Orvis pajamas, and slipping under the covers without waking the dogs, a technique in which all anthropologists receive extensive training because getting into a bed with a snack in the presence of pug dogs is tantamount to getting naked, basting yourself in honey, and lying down on a fire ant hill.

"What?" you ask. "You didn't bring a pen and a notebook?"

Of course not. Were you whelped in a barn or something? A gentleman never takes notes in bed.

> *I saluted my decision by opening a package of trail mix... The sound accompanying this event detonated a chain reaction.*

In anthropological circles, the importance of looking earnest is exceeded only by the importance of sounding earnest. Therefore, we must now turn our attention to the secrets of constructing keen insights out of ordinary canine behavior—or out of thin air, if need be. Other than a flair for accessorizing, there is no research skill more critical to success; and the secrets of obtaining this skill, I might add, are not available in stores.

Nor is the kind of patience required for thoroughgoing research. I made this discovery when I ventured to the kitchen to begin studying my dogs, only to realize that my work would be delayed because most of the dogs were sleeping, as usual, in a pile under one of the kitchen chairs—except for Burt and Harry, who were sleeping in a smaller pile in the spacious crate in the bedroom a short distance away.

The West Goshen Pug School synchronized swim team takes a break from rehearsals.

While I was waiting for the dogs to wake up and do something social, I drafted an official statement of purpose for my investigation. Some researchers prefer the more traditional approach—i.e., gathering their data before deciding what it's supposed to demonstrate. I, however, had found a tidy statement of purpose in *The Social Lives of Dogs* and decided that I, too, would try to arrive at "some notion of what our animals were thinking, to get glimpses of their worldviews, and to understand their longings." In addition, I would present techniques that enable you to look and sound as if you know what you're talking about even when you don't.

I saluted my decision by opening a package of trail mix, a survival tool that no self-respecting anthropologist should stay home without. The sound accompanying this event detonated a chain reaction. The first five links of the chain sprang into a full-tilt begging frenzy, bouncing around like mechanized pogo sticks, tongues flapping from side to side, eyes threatening to pop out of their sockets. This, in turn, set Burt and Harry to howling.

"There they go again," I said, shaking my head ruefully. "Whatever can they be howling about?"

Quicker than a pug will seize upon an errant raisin from a bag of trail mix, the answer came to me: Burt's and Harry's paging of the other members of the pack for information regarding the trail mix was obviously part of the rich, nuanced social existence from which pack members draw emotional succor as well as information critical to their survival.

If you're thinking that you'd never be able to derive such keen, learned inferences from watching your dogs' behavior, remember two things. First, the number of ways to interpret behavior is equal to or greater than the number of persons observing that behavior. Second, the more fanciful the assertion, the more difficult it is to disprove.

Elizabeth Marshall Thomas demonstrates a mastery of these principles throughout *The Social Lives of Dogs*. After watching her dogs on their constitutional walks, she concluded that social hierarchy determines where dogs in a pack choose to relieve themselves. Indeed, writes Thomas, the lowest-ranking pack member carefully chooses the spot the other dogs will mark.

When I first encountered this observation, I was awed by Thomas' ability to read her dogs' behavior. I also wondered why my dogs didn't behave like hers. If the older members of my pack deferred to the newest members in selecting a target, they'd all be urinating on the corner of the fridge or the rug in front of the sink. What's more, whenever I take the dogs outside, they scatter like politicians the day after Congress adjourns. Why, I asked myself, did Thomas' dogs conduct a close-order drill while mine engaged in a veritable crapshoot?

The enormity of this question might have caused a lesser person to fold up his or her bag of trail mix and quit the observation post, but I decided that even if my dogs couldn't emulate the way Thomas' dogs behave, I could at least have a go at making keen, learned inferences. Thus, I decided that my dogs' preference for individual over group marking was a clear indication that the observance of social distance among pugs is more finely developed than it is among other breeds, which, no doubt, is a consequence of pugs' clear preference for people over members of their own species.

The ability to make this sort of inference is all that stands between the average dog owner, lolling about staring vacantly at his or her dogs, and the best-selling author at a book signing where dog owners loll about and stare at the author. Accordingly, it would be instructive to consider another example of the fine art of shooting from the lip.

Thomas claims that dogs "are very much like people in their social placements...the point at which a person enters a group determines his social position. Dogs are much the same. Many people who acquire a second dog observe that the first dog continues to outrank the new dog even if the new dog is bigger and stronger."

Once again, my pugs do not adhere to this paradigm. The newest members of the group will challenge any other member, and if, as we noted earlier in this monograph, there is no sound more ludicrous than the sound of pug dogs howling, the runner-up has to be the sound of two pugs fighting. As often as I've heard that cacophony, it never fails to startle me—until I remember that pugs weren't forged in the crucible of warfare. Pug fanciers' collective desire for a neonatal face and a cookie-jar figure in their dogs may have wrought unhealthy consequences in the breed, but that desire has also rendered pugs incapable of inflicting anything more serious than drool on their opponents.

Indeed, that's how we determine the winner of any dustup in our house—by assessing the drool on each combatant's coat. This being a family-oriented publication, I won't detail the scientific formulae that underlie such a calculation, except to note that it does involve multiple regression equations. Suffice it to say that after we have determined which dog's coat contains the most drool by atomic volume, we declare the other dog the winner, and the rest of the pack settle up whatever side bets they may have made on the contest.

As the various authors of a certain series of instructional books are wont to say, the "least you need to know" about anthropological research is this: the principal that says interpretation is in the eye of the beholder is reinforced by the principal that says no matter what interpretations you attach to your dogs' behavior, they aren't going to contradict you. People might think you're a few beans shy of a burrito, but so what? Should anyone challenge your assumptions about your dogs' behavior, imply archly that the person is a hide-bound traditionalist—then ask him or her to prove that dogs don't experience *déjà vu* or can't tell when another dog is having a birthday.

Once you've mastered the challenging riposte, you needn't be intimidated any longer by people who know more or work harder than you do. You can contradict anybody, anytime, anywhere—as long as you're careful to look and sound as if you know what you're talking about.

Chapter 16

The Pug Dog's Top-Eleven Lists

From the Ten Commandments to David Letterman's Top Ten lists, human history is dotted with information packaged in tidy groups of ten: the ten-second quiz, the ten-minute recipe, ten secrets to lasting weight loss. When the question is presentation, the answer is often expressed in the power of ten.

Melvil Dewey, who was born of the tenth of December 1851, appreciated this fact. His Dewey Decimal Classification system, which he created when he was a twenty-one-year-old library assistant at Amherst College, is used in 95 percent of all public and school libraries in the United States today. Dewey's system is also used in more than 135 countries around the world and as a browsing mechanism for locating resources on the World Wide Web.

So enduring is the appeal of Dewey's creation that the Missouri River Regional Library in Jefferson City, Missouri, employs a friendly-looking cartoon mutt called Dewey the Decimal Dog as a mascot. Although Dewey makes an engaging pitchman, the folks at the Missouri River Regional Library must be unaware that dogs employ a different numerical system than we humans do. Following careful research and observation, I have concluded that my pugs use a base-eleven counting scheme, which illustrates their penchant for thinking outside the library as well as their fascination with prime numbers.

The higher-order quantum mathematics that I used to arrive at this conclusion need not bedevil us here. Suffice it to say that my discovery has several practical applications for pug owners. For example, the pug's preference for a base-eleven numerical system means that you're wasting your breath if you yell "I'll give you ten seconds to stop that" when you discover your pugs trying to break into the trash container in the kitchen.

> *The pug's employment of a base-eleven numerical system also adds a new wrinkle to the standard top-ten list.*

The pug's employment of a base-eleven numerical system also adds a new wrinkle to the standard top-ten list. Consequently, while mulling over the most riveting pug questions of the moment—why pugs should not be allowed to have cell phones, how to tell if the person you're talking to in a chatroom is really a pug, and which things should never happen to a pug—I realized that for the sake of solidarity with my subject I should present eleven rather than ten items in response to each of these questions.

Eleven Reasons Pugs Shouldn't Have Cell Phones

Several years ago Keiji Tachikawa, the president of Japan's NTT Mobile Communications Network, announced his intention to equip dogs, cats, bicycles, and vending machines with mobile phones. Worried that everybody past the age of toilet training in Japan would soon own a cell phone—and keenly aware that a saturated market lifts no boats—Tachikawa declared, "We have to target everything that moves."

Although Tachikawa expected the Japanese cell-phone market to grow to 360 million contracts by 2005, he predicted that the mobile phone as we know it—affixed to the ear of a soccer mom in a minivan blocking traffic in the middle of an intersection—would account for only one-third of those contracts. The majority of the new subscriptions would be for cars (one hundred million), bicycles (sixty million), laptop computers (fifty million), and household pets (twenty million), with another ten million subscriptions coming from ships, motorbikes, and vending machines.

As all-inclusive as Tachikawa's marketing vision was, it did not include every possible location in which mobile phones might be deployed. I suggest, therefore, that mobile phones should be

A member of the Queen's Royal Guard is taunted by a young puppy into breaking formation.

available in churches, in case you have to call a lawyer to plea-bargain your penance when you go to confession; in public restrooms, in the event that there are interesting numbers on the walls; and on all counters in large department stores, in case you need to report a missing sales clerk.

Tachikawa maintained that dogs should be outfitted with mobile phones because "depending how your dog barks, you could tell whether it is in an emergency or not." That kind of suggestion might lead a person to suspect that Tachikawa's bottom line is in the midst of an emergency—or that he's never owned a dog. We can think of at least eleven good reasons why a dog, especially a pug dog, should not have a cell phone.

11. Shows off by talking on phone while hanging his head out the car window.

10. Makes Prince-Albert-in-a-can calls to people named "Katz."

9. Rings you at work and barks to remind you that it's almost dinner time.

8. Runs up $500 phone bill calling psychics at 1-900-DOG-STAR.

7. Greedy phone companies increase hidden rover rates.

6. MCI and Sprint pester you about switching your dog's long distance account.

5. Forwards his calls to your number before taking a nap in the yard.

4. Hounds the Lucky Dog phone company about a job.

3. Would add way too many Maxs and Pals to the phone book.

2. It's humiliating to be put on hold by a dog.

1. The cat will want one soon.

Eleven Ways to Sniff Out Pugs Online

The First Principle of Electronic Communication was defined in a cartoon in the July 5, 1993, edition of the *New Yorker*. There are two dogs in the cartoon. One, who is seated at a desk in front of a computer, is saying to the other, "On the Internet no one knows you're a dog."

"On the Internet no one knows you're a dog."

This cartoon is often cited by social critics and other scolds eager to sound the alarm about the dangers of taking people at face value when we can't see their faces. Such advice falls squarely into the don't-dump-scalding-coffee-on-your-lap category: it's helpful to a point, but it lacks nuance.

Obviously, people should be told that a rendezvous at the Hour Glass Motel with somebody called The Love Muffin, whom they've just met online, isn't a four-star idea. Nevertheless, after a person has internalized that bit of personal safety advice, she or he still faces overriding challenges: how does one separate the men from the mutts, the women from the woofers, online? How do you avoid the heartbreak of showing up for scones and chai at some tony establishment with the requisite nature prints on the wall only to find that the person you're supposed to meet there is drinking from a bowl?

In order to help people avoid that sticky wicket, I have prepared the Sirius Internet Fabrication Test (SIFT), a precision psychometric instrument designed to keep the wag from tailing a dog.

Readers are advised to turn two enthusiastic dewclaws down on the urge to get better acquainted with anyone who lights up the SIFT scoreboard on more than two of the following eleven items, all of which suggest that the person you're talking to in a chat room is really a pug.

11. Chat room name is *Pugsley* or *Lady.*

10. Insists on meeting at PetSmart instead of a restaurant.

9. Only measures height to the shoulders.

8. Wants to know how old you are in dog years.

7. Thinks the "pause" button on the keyboard is misspelled.

6. Asks repeatedly if you've been fixed.

5. Acts weird about exchanging photos.

4. Just had the entire house re-roofed for $100.

3. Asks if you thought *Men in Black II* was better than the original.

2. Can't understand why people make such a fuss about having quintuplets.

1. Shows unusual interest in the schedule of "the e-mailman."

Eleven Things That Shouldn't Happen to a Pug

Tales of pestilence and woe frequently include the observation "It shouldn't happen to a dog." In the afterglow of the Clinton-Lewinsky intrigue, for example, an irate moralist complained to the *Dayton Daily News*, "What has happened to our president shouldn't happen to a dog. How would you like to have your life put on the Internet? It's despicable, and so is the media."

The irate moralist might take some comfort in knowing that what goes around comes around, and our former president, to be sure, was on the giving as well as the receiving end of this dogged expression. "What Clinton does to [writers] Joe Klein and Bill Safire shouldn't happen to a dog," said Roger Rosenblatt in *Time* on the occasion of Clinton's second inauguration. "None of these first-class intelligences are normally subject to fits of rage or blue funks, but when it comes to the man from Hope, whoa Nellie."

The list of things that shouldn't happen to a dog forms an interesting cul-de-sac in the public discourse. According to finance writer Jane Bryant Quinn, "What happens to whistle-blowers in this country shouldn't happen to a dog." Screenwriter Stephen Schiff believes that "Having a lawyer in the editing room is something that shouldn't happen to a dog." *Men's Health* magazine assures us that certain kinds of foot problems shouldn't happen to a dog, and the Federal Communications Commission avers that slamming long-distance phone customers—a practice wherein a provider transfers a customer's account to another provider without first obtaining that customer's consent—shouldn't happen to a dog either. Ironically, this did happen to a dog when Qwest Communications International forged a customer's signature in order to pass him to another provider—only to discover that the customer had signed up for service in his dog's name.

"It shouldn't happen to a dog," which is believed to be Yiddish in derivation, has served as the title of a book, a movie, and an episode of *Bewitched*. I haven't seen or read any of these yet, but I have heard the expression "It shouldn't happen to a dog" often enough to realize that many of the things people believe "shouldn't happen to a dog" are actually things that shouldn't happen to people. Why would a dog care if there were a lawyer in the editing room or if details of a tryst with the dog next door wound up on the Internet?

This is not to say there aren't things that shouldn't happen to a dog. Unfortunately, however, we humans tend toward speciesism in thought as well as deed, and our kennel blindness causes us to overlook some of the truly shocking misfortunes that shouldn't happen to a dog. In order to correct that imbalance I present here eleven things that truly shouldn't happen to a pug.

11. Electronic fence collar becomes sensitive to the Oprah satellite.

10. New ID tag displays a sell-by date.

9. Starts to look like owner, who resembles Jonathan Winters.

8. Starts to look like female owner, who resembles Jonathan Winters.

7. Somebody dumps a transistorized dog on doorstep; owners decide to keep it.

6. Cat learns to program doggie door.

5. Encounters chalk drawing of flattened self on the sidewalk while walking with owner.

4. Owner's new boyfriend lifts leg around the house.

3. Home security alarm goes off five minutes after owners go out to take in a movie.

2. Starts to look people-eared.

1. Picture taken with Santa shows up on a milk carton.

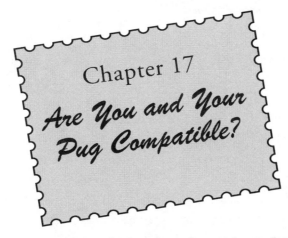

Chapter 17

Are You and Your Pug Compatible?

Some people contend that the longer we live with our dogs the more we come to resemble them, but I don't put much stock in this theory. Even though I bore a certain resemblance to pugs before I acquired my first one—I had a low center of gravity, a big head, and short legs—I don't look any more like a pug now than I did then, and that was twelve years ago. Like my dogs', my chin whiskers have gone a tad white in the meantime, but you could still distinguish me from any of my six pugs in a police lineup.

One lazy afternoon as I was wondering how this look-alike theory had sprouted legs, my thoughts strayed to a related question: do people who live with dogs for any length of time begin to resemble them temperamentally? If so, I had an edge in that category, too: I wilt in the heat; I view exercise with disdain; and I'll eat anything that doesn't sport a surgeon general's warning or a sell-by date more than nine months past due.

As I often do when I have a soul-searching question, I turned to the Internet. There I discovered a quiz entitled "What Breed of Dog Are You?" on the Emode.com Web site (www.emode.com). The quiz contained fifteen multiple-choice questions that wanted to know, among other things, which of several foods I would eat for lunch every day for the rest of my life if I had to, whether I think life is too short to drink cheap wine, and how much time I spend getting ready to go out.

After answering the questions as though I were under oath, I clicked the "submit" button, happily expecting to be informed that I am a pug in human clothing. Unhappily, I received the following cheerful message instead: "No bones about it, you're a friendly, easy-going basset hound…you treasure the moments when you don't have anything on your agenda except plopping down on the couch for a night of 'Must-See TV'…some folks might misinterpret your relaxed attitude and lifestyle as laziness, but those who really know you think your no-frills approach to life is refreshing."

Horrified, I looked around quickly to see if any of the six pugs lounging in the kitchen, where I was Web-browsing on my laptop, could view the screen. As usual they were asleep, so I quietly reviewed my answers to the Emode quiz.

After the shock of discovering that I'm a basset hound had begun to wear off, indignation set in.

I wasn't spoofing when I said "not much" is the amount of time I spend getting ready to go out. I was certain that "never" describes the possibility of my singing in a karaoke bar. I know for damn sure I'd rather be a socialite than a bus driver, grade school teacher, or any of the other vocational choices on the test. Indeed, I'd rather be a socialite than anything in the world—except a semiretired freelance writer who works at home with six pugs and seven cats for company.

Nevertheless, there was no denying that the description of a basset hound fit me like a DNA profile. The $114 a month I was sending to my cable company at the time speaks to my affection for television, and my all-purpose wardrobe—jeans, baggy shirts, and Birkenstocks—bears witness to my no-frills approach to life.

After the shock of discovering that I'm a basset hound had begun to wear off, indignation set in. As a matter of fact, I was so indignant that I decided to take the Emode True Talent Test, which purported to ascertain where my true talent lies. I had taken similar tests before, and apart from the one that said I was best suited for a life of crime, every one identified verbal skills as my strong—and in many cases my only—suit. If Emode told me anything different, I could safely ignore the results of my personality test and go on believing that I am a pug in human clothing.

The direction of the letters told Poirot there was a dyslexic pug trapped inside the snow-covered van.

No such luck. The Emode True Talent Test smarmily informed me, "Your verbal knowledge can make you versatile in expressing yourself."

Stuck between a rock and a keyboard, I wondered if I was the only pug owner in the world whose better canine half was another breed. What I know about the Law of Large Numbers and the Big Bang theory told me I was not. Next I wondered if I might get a book chapter out of this topic. What I know about spinning any subject into a sixteen-hundred-word essay told me that I could. Therefore, I determined to devise my own compatibility quiz: a rigorously scientific instrument that didn't contain nonessential questions about wine, karaoke bars, or lunch choices; a test that will truly determine if pugs and their owners are compatible.

The Pug Compatibility Predictor

Part I: About Your Pug

Answer the following questions as you think your pug would answer them if he or she had just been given a large injection of truth serum.

1. I'm at my best when the house is rocking and someone carries me around the room singing "This Old Man."
   Yes   Maybe Yes/(Maybe No)   Certainly Not

3 2. I yawn, therefore I am.
   (Yes)   Maybe Yes/Maybe No   Certainly Not

 3. Mick Jagger looks more sexy the more wrinkled he gets.
   Yes   Maybe Yes/Maybe No   (Certainly Not)

4. I prefer to ride in a car than to chase one.
   Yes   Maybe Yes/Maybe No   (Certainly Not)

3 5. The vacuum cleaner is the spawn of Satan.
   (Yes)   Maybe Yes/Maybe No   Certainly Not

3 6. I become depressed if my owner sits in his or her favorite chair without me.
   (Yes)   Maybe Yes/Maybe No   Certainly Not

7. Some of my best friends are cats.
   (Yes)   Maybe Yes/Maybe No   Certainly Not

3 8. I never met a snack I didn't like.
   (Yes)   Maybe Yes/Maybe No   Certainly Not

3 9. I'd sooner play with poisonous snakes on amphetamines than pee outside when it's raining.
   (Yes)   Maybe Yes/Maybe No   Certainly Not

3 10. I like to relax by having my nails done.
   Yes   Maybe Yes/Maybe No   (Certainly Not)

Scoring: For questions numbered 1 through 6, 8, and 9, award three points for each Yes answer; for question 7 award three points for answering Maybe Yes/Maybe No; for question 10 award three points for answering Certainly Not.

Part II: About You

Answer the following questions as you think you would answer them if you weren't deluding yourself.

1. A dog is a dog, but a pug is another person in the house.
   (Yes)   Maybe Yes/Maybe No   Certainly Not

2. Only the most backward countries refuse to allow dogs in restaurants.
   Yes   Maybe Yes/(Maybe No)   Certainly Not

3. Waking up without a pug in bed is like waking up on the wrong side of the toilet.
   Yes   Maybe Yes/Maybe No   (Certainly Not)

4. My expression never betrays what I'm thinking.
   (Yes)   Maybe Yes/Maybe No   Certainly Not

5. A handshake is as good as a hug.
   Yes   Maybe Yes/Maybe No   (Certainly Not)

6. There is no three-second rule regarding spilled food.
   Yes   Maybe Yes/Maybe No   (Certainly Not)

7. I would rather have a root canal from a nearsighted dentist with delirium tremens than make a speech.
   (Yes)   Maybe Yes/Maybe No   Certainly Not

8. Good moats make good neighbors.
   Yes   Maybe Yes/Maybe No   (Certainly Not)

9. I am always the first person to leave a party, even if I'm hosting it.
   Yes   Maybe Yes/Maybe No   (Certainly Not)

10. There is more grass between the bricks in my patio than in my back yard.
    Yes   (Maybe Yes/Maybe No)   Certainly Not

Scoring: For questions numbered 1 through 3, 6, and 10, award three points for each Yes answer. For questions numbered 4, 5, and 7 through 9, award three points for each Certainly Not answer.

Your pug's score _____ 18 _____ Your score 15 _____

The Requisite Discussion

Outgoing (30-21). People scoring in this range believe that the examined life is not worth living. Their idea of a quiet night at home is to invite a dozen of their closest friends over to watch television and spend the night. Pugs scoring in this range go into a state of ecstasy whenever they hear the doorbell ring.

Ongoing (18-9). People and pugs scoring in this category enjoy socializing, especially around holidays, but also need time alone to meditate, recharge their batteries, and experience the wonder of being in the moment.

Ingoing (6-0). People who barely move the needle are the kind for whom soup for one and single-slot toothbrush holders were invented. Pugs in this range are so shy they never let humans see them eating.

Interpreting Your Score

The closer you and your pug score on the Pug Compatibility Predictor, the more happy you are likely to be. If both of you score above twenty, for example, your open-house weekends and frequent dinner parties won't drive your pug into analysis, nor will your pug's fondness for games in which you have to participate cause you to spend your weekends in an ashram.

> *The closer you and your pug score on the Pug Compatibility Predictor, the more happy you are likely to be.*

On the other side of the mirror, if you and your pug score in the single digits, you both believe that being alone is preferable to being lonely in a crowd, and the odds are good that you will enjoy being alone together. Each of you is content to listen to the music of your own soul as you while away the hours in solitary pursuits. What's more, you'll be understanding if your pug would rather sit in its own bed than on your lap, and your pug won't take offense if you prefer to shake hands with it rather than pet it.

Of course, middle-of-the-road scores by you and your pug are also predictive of a cheerful relationship.

A Breed Apart?

What if your score is in a different zip code from your pug's? What if you're a thirty, and she's a nine? Does this mean you're bound to wind up on Jerry Springer? Not necessarily, unless both of you have exceedingly bad hair and no makeup skills. If you and your pug are coexisting peacefully despite the difference in your scores, you have obviously repaired—or have learned to avoid—the significant potholes in your relationship. If you stick to the main roads and observe the speed limit, your journey through life together can be a pleasant one.

Chapter 18
Country Comforts

Time seldom passes more slowly than when you're stuck behind a school bus on a narrow country road at 4:15 in the afternoon. The same scholars who zoom past you in the mall, a blur of baggy clothes in mutant colors, turn suddenly deliberate as the big yellow taxi creeps to a halt near their driveways. They shuffle across the road at arthritic speed, pausing to wave or to shout insults at the same fellow travelers with whom they were fighting forty-five seconds ago. Consequently, the average person living in the country spends the equivalent of five child-exiting years mired in a simmering funk behind lurching school buses. Realtors don't tell you that when they get to the safer-schools part of their house-and-pony demonstrations.

"School kids walking," I muttered sullenly one recent afternoon as I came to a halt behind a school bus on Little Conestoga Road. In less time than it takes Larry King to shill whatever nutritional supplement he's pimping for this week, the bus had already stopped twice. "They named this damn road accurately," I groused. "Wagon trains made better time along here than I do. I should have known better than to stop for coffee." With a malevolent sigh I reached for the grande-sized container of joe that warned me in two languages about the potential of its contents to bring pain and suffering to one's nether regions if spilled upon them.

About then I noticed the front door of a house on the left-hand side of the road opening slightly. It wasn't one of those offensively huge executive homes that burst forth like alien, body-snatching pods on perfectly innocent hillsides in these parts. It was instead a modest, dignified, older house, a little-house-on-the-prairie-type house. Out of this premodern, nondescript white house toddled a plain, nondescript dog that looked old enough to remember when farms ruled the roost in these parts, which wasn't all that long ago.

There was a smile on the dog's face and a measured wag in her tail as two children crossed the road in front of the school bus and started through the yard toward the porch where the old dog was waiting. She didn't go bounding off the porch or anything ostentatious like Lassie or one of those Hollywood showoff dogs would have done. She was of an age where a dog learns to pick its spots for displays of unbridled enthusiasm, but you could tell—if you had half an eye for such things—that she was happy to see her young friends nonetheless, glad to have them back from their adventures in the world beyond the yard.

"[Shoot]," I said to myself, an unbidden, sappy grin oozing its way across my face. "That's nice."

A horn sounded behind me, and I noticed that the school bus had lurched its way forward while I had been lost in Rockwell land. "And the horse you rode in on, pal," I mumbled, shooting the driver of the car behind me the evil eye in the rearview mirror. I caught up to the school bus, which had stopped again about fifteen yards down the road to discharge four more children. As they crossed the road to their house, another old dog, nondescript and mixed-breed like the first but salt-and-pepper instead of tan, sauntered down the driveway to greet them. The two smaller children, first or second graders, raced past the dog to some unutterably important business. The dog didn't seem to mind or to take their haste personally. She continued on to the two older children, who scarcely paid her any more mind. She didn't seem to take that personally either, although their failure to give her more than a perfunctory pat on the head did take a little of the curl out of her tail. She fell in step beside them all the same as they continued up the drive, content to play whatever role she would be assigned in their afternoon.

At this point I was awash in gee-golly-wow endorphins, and I would have followed that creeping school bus for half an hour just

All higher cultures arrange time according to a solar year or a lunar year. Fetch is a proponent of the lunar approach.

to see those scenes repeated a few more times. Why not? I still had three-quarters of a grande-sized container of potentially scalding coffee in the rack and nine CDs in the changer that I hadn't listened to yet. These comforting scenes were like organic, free-range Prozac for the soul following a few days in which not much had gone right and I was beginning to believe that a friend of mine was correct when he said "The trouble with people is they're just no damn good."

Unfortunately, the school bus turned off into a development after one more stop, that one dogless. I felt sorry for the kid who got off the bus without any dog to greet him. I hoped he had a cat inside sleeping on the bed. I further hoped that his wasn't, as mine had been, a no-pets-allowed childhood. Those plastic soldiers that were the after-school companions of my youth were better at holding a stay than most dogs are, but I've yet to see a toy soldier pacing back and forth on a front porch—at least when I was sober—anticipating anyone's arrival. I resolved that the next time I was feeling sorry for myself I'd hie on down to the south end of Little Conestoga Road about 4:15 in the afternoon and follow the school bus for a while.

With the homecoming scenes hanging in the air like wood-smoke from a beneficent fire, I continued along to the village where we live. There wasn't any dog shuffling down to the end of the driveway to greet me, but as the van drew even with the side porch a flock of pug dogs sleeping in the backyard burst into life and raced to the fence, hopping up and down and barking, demanding to know where I had been, why I had taken so long, and what I had bought them.

Although I hadn't been lucky enough to have a dog when I was a kid, I am six-times-over lucky today with half-a-dozen scampering pugs dancing attendance on my comings and goings. What's more, I'm old enough to drive the bus, so it never leaves without me no matter how long I dawdle when I'm supposed to be somewhere.

After I had walked the dogs around the yard for a few minutes, I took them inside and parceled out the treats I had bought for them on my trip to the supermarket. As I did, I hummed the refrain of an Elton John song: "And it's good old country comforts in my bones, just the sweetest sound my ears have ever known, just an old-fashioned feeling in my bones, country comforts and the road that's goin' home."

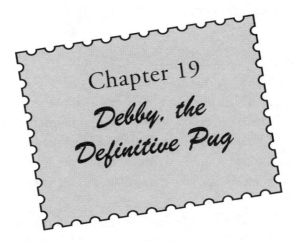

Chapter 19
Debby, the Definitive Pug

The word *pug* first appeared in the English language in the mid-1500s as a term of endearment applied to persons but rarely to animals. During the next fifty years *pug* acquired two additional meanings—*courtesan* and *bargeman*—which are strange bedfellows, at least linguistically. By 1664 *pug* also meant *demon, imp, sprite, monkey,* and *ape*. Not until the middle of the next century, however, did *pug* come to mean "a dwarf breed of dog resembling a bull-dog in miniature." *The Oxford English Dictionary,* which recorded that meaning, also noted that the pug "on account of its affectionate nature [was] much kept as a pet."

No pug of my acquaintance personified more of the various meanings of *pug* as impishly or demonically as Debby. Deb's registered name was *Ivanwold You Light Up My Life*. I thought at first it was the clumsiest name ever hung on a dog, but the more I became acquainted with Debby's crustiness and grit, her courtesan wiles and bargeman attitude, the more I appreciated the irony in naming such a salty dog after such a cloying song—and then choosing the first name of the song's perpetrator, Debby Boone, for a nickname.

As I have recounted in Chapter 2, Debby was an irrepressible bad-hat of a dog, a trait that gave her a leg up in my affections because my favorite people and dogs have always been bad hats. Debby never let us cut her nails without a fight, and she seldom let us eat without making us share our food with her. She chased the cats just to watch them run, and she was wont to sneak upstairs to go truffle hunting in their litter pan. When she was finished, she often left a truffle or two of her own on the rug to express her disdain for lower species, which included all other living creatures except my wife Mary Ann and me.

Debby was eleven months old when she came to live with us in July 1991. We drove eleven hundred miles from our house in southeastern Pennsylvania to Tampa, Florida, to pick her up because the weather was too hot to permit shipping her by plane. After spending a few days in Florida, we drove back home in our Geo Storm crammed with luggage, a cat cage with a Persian inside, my computer, and our other pug, Percy. Debby amused herself the entire way by nudging Percy off the lap of whoever wasn't driving, peering out the window for a few moments, quitting her post to root around in the car's crowded interior, then returning to her lap perch as soon as Percy had made bold enough to attempt to occupy it again. We began to suspect we had a handful of dog on our hands.

> We began to suspect we had a handful of dog on our hands.

Debby confirmed that suspicion minutes after we had arrived home. Having logged all those miles in the car—a distance she had made seem twice as long as it was—Debby must have considered the car her house, for when Mary Ann started off for the post office to collect the mail while I stayed in the yard with Debby and Percy, Debby went flying after the car. Mary Ann had to jump out and stop traffic in the street, where Debby had raced in pursuit of the car. The next day we arranged to have the yard fenced.

We had never considered fencing the yard when Percy was the only pug in residence because he never strayed more than three feet from my wife or me. Indeed, we had to be careful not to stop too suddenly when we walked, otherwise we'd feel Percy's nose bumping against the backs of our legs.

In October that year we were at a dog show in Charlottesville, Virginia, when a woman approached us and asked excitedly, "Is that Debby?" We said yes, and the woman, who lived in Ohio, informed us that she had whelped and raised Debby for the people from whom we had gotten her in Florida. They were simply Debby's breeders of record.

"I cried for days when I had to send that puppy to Florida," the woman said. She told us that Deb had been the only puppy in her litter that survived, which didn't surprise us, and that Deb had been raised by herself in a large room. One wall of that room had doors at either end outfitted with baby gates. Those doors led to other rooms, where other puppies lived. Debby thought it great sport to race to the gate at one doorway and hurl insults at the dogs in that room until they started barking angrily. Then she would race to the gate at the other doorway and stir up the dogs in that room. She ran from one gate to the other, keeping the dogs in both rooms in turmoil, until she tired of this game.

A month after the Charlottesville show I took Debby to Virginia Beach for a four-day cluster of shows. I was working on a proposal for my first book then—a how-to manual for new or prospective owners of Scottish fold cats—so I intended to use the time between shows to get some writing done. I had never been anywhere with only a dog for company before, and I was amazed at what fine company this dog was. She certainly had a way of lighting up an outing, but whenever I left her in the room for any reason, she made this strangulated, you're-breaking-my-poor-little-dog-heart noise to let me know what a wretch I was. When I returned to the room, she would be waiting near the door. I realized then that she had me by the heart.

The feeling was reinforced later in the month after Debby came down with a cold that quickly degenerated into pneumonia despite prompt treatment with antibiotics from our vet. When Deb's condition worsened after two days' treatment, we took her to a second vet who told us she wouldn't be going home that night. This vet explained that he planned to quadruple her diuretic and put her on intravenous antibiotics and fluids. I don't recall whether he used the words *life threatening*, but I certainly didn't want to contemplate the threat of life without this pushy, beguiling dog. On the way back home, despite Percy's best efforts to console me, I had to stop in the parking lot of a convenience store to regain my composure.

We were allowed to visit Debby two days later. We arrived with Percy in tow and half a pound of turkey breast from the delicatessen at the same convenience store where I'd stopped on the way home from the vet's. When Debby fell on the turkey, polished it off, and then tried to dominate Percy by putting her front legs on his shoulders, we fairly broke into cheers. She was released from the hospital the next day, as ornery as she'd ever been and even more deeply entrenched in our hearts.

...Debby gave birth to her first and last litter of puppies in April 1992. Not surprisingly, she refused to acknowledge maternity.

As I have recounted also in Chapter 2, Debby gave birth to her first and last litter of puppies in April 1992. Not surprisingly, she refused to acknowledge maternity. The puppies, two girls, were obliged to grow up virtually without a mother while Mary Ann and I were obliged to go without uninterrupted sleep for nearly a month, during which time we got up at regular—and too brief— intervals throughout the night to affix each of Debby's daughters to a nipple and stand guard while they nursed. Deb's rejection of motherhood and the luxating patella (trick knee) she developed while she was pregnant insured that she wasn't bred again.

Debby's daughter Patty and Patty's daughter June were bred, however, and by September of 1996 our pug family had grown to eight. At about that time I noticed two dark blotches of pigment making their way across Debby's eyes. I had written a book about pugs by then—a book inspired in large part by this wonderful dog—and I recognized her condition as pigmentary keratitis, an affliction in which the eye lays down a rogue layer of pigment in response to irritation and/or insufficient tearing.

Debby's eyes didn't respond to treatment. Eventually she would be blind. I had read on the Internet about an operation in which the top layer of the cornea is stripped away to restore a dog's sight. I figured when Deb's vision got bad, she would have that surgery.

The pug's motto, Multum in parvo, is a Latin phrase that means "a lot of dog in a little space."

By the time Deb was seven, she was also troubled by arthritis as a consequence of her knee operation. Rimadyl® and Glyco-Flex® worked wonders for that condition, and she still enjoyed running up and down the fence barking at the dog next door. Because of her medical problems and her seniority—and because she was dedicated to living life on her own schedule—we stopped requiring her to go along every time the other dogs were ushered out for lavatory breaks. If she looked at us as though to say "not now," we let her stay inside, often reinforcing her behavior with a snack.

One summer day in 1998, Debby walked into the door jamb while going outside. Keratitis had turned her world to shadows. Before long, even though she could still follow the other dogs out the door, she stood in the driveway and cocked her head to one side while they raced toward the yard. When we called her, she gamely followed the sound of our voices into the yard. She still navigated well indoors and was still capable of putting her front paws on our legs while we were eating, demanding her share. I felt sorry for her whenever I gave the dogs treats because she knew what was going on but couldn't see well enough to get into the scrum. By using a little misdirection and tossing a treat to the right or left, I was able to distract the other dogs and give Deb her treat and, because I never could resist her, a little extra.

At three in the morning that October 15, Debby had a seizure. By the time we got her to the emergency hospital an hour away, her temperature was 105. The diagnosis was hypoglycemia, most

She would never be her young self again, but even her old self could light up a life.

likely brought on by a pancreatic tumor. When we picked her up the next afternoon, she was a sight. The lower portion of both her front legs had been shaved, and she was having a mild seizure. There was confusion on her sightless face, and it killed me to see it there.

With Prednisone and extra meals each day, Debby was soon her old self. She would never be her young self again, but even her old self could light up a life. We settled into a pleasant routine: after the dogs had gone outside at four each morning and had been stashed in the kitchen, Deb got to go back to our bed, where we gave her a snack to tide her over until breakfast. Each morning around eleven, I'd stop whatever I was working on, open a small can of dog food, and empty it into a bowl. At the sound of the can opener, Deb raced to the gate separating the kitchen from the hallway, and after I'd opened the gate, she charged down the hall to the spot where I fed her in our bedroom.

We had been told Debby should have an ultrasound exam to see if she did have a pancreatic tumor, but we put that off for a spell. Pancreatic tumors are rarely benign, and if they can be operated on—a procedure that we weren't sure we wanted to put Debby through—they're apt to grow back anyway. Besides, Debby was acting so lively and enjoying all the extra attention so much, I imagined we'd have that light in our lives a while longer; but just past midnight on the day after I'd finally scheduled an ultrasound, she had another seizure. Mary Ann fed her some Karo syrup and dog food, and the seizure seemed to abate; but in the time it took to go turn out the lights in the kitchen, Debby was convulsing again.

We called our vet. She said she would let the folks at the emergency hospital know we were coming. As soon as we hung up, we realized there was no point in subjecting this game curmudgeon of a dog to further misery. When we had taken her to the hospital following her first seizure, which wasn't anywhere near this severe, her temperature had spiked to 105. The vet who had examined her then said Deb was near death. We feared that in the hour it would take us to get to the hospital, Debby would be gone. We decided to spare her any further suffering. We called our vet back and said we were bringing Debby over to have her put to sleep. At the end of a somber three-mile drive to the vet's office, Debby was so shaken by seizures that the bottom of her tongue was bleeding where it had scraped against her teeth.

Normally that would have left me blubbering, but I was consumed by rage. I was too furious to cry, too resentful at my helplessness. I watched stone-faced as Mary Ann held Debby on the examining table to steady her while the vet slid the needle into Debby's leg. By the time the fluid had run its deadly course, there was one fine dog lying dead on the table, her tongue hanging out as though she had been caught in midstride trying to outrun the devil.

We had had to have one of our cats put to sleep four days before, and when our vet asked at that time if we had ever seen euthanasia, I replied, "Yes, but don't they usually have a buffet?" This time there weren't any jokes.

On the way home Mary Ann began to say something about putting Debby to sleep being the right thing to do. "I don't want to talk about it," I snapped.

"Well, I might," Mary Ann said calmly.

"Then call somebody up. I've got writing to do. I'm going home and getting to work."

I was still in a murderous fury when we got home. I went to work on an assignment that was due that day. I would show God or the universe or whoever took my dog from me: "You might have taken my dog, but it isn't going to bother me. I'm OK, even if your [screwed]-up world isn't."

Around four o'clock, just about the time Debby usually woke us up to take her outside, my resolve crumbled. It was devastating how a house with seven dogs and seven cats in it could still seem so empty.

Chapter 20

A Dog Runs Through It

People who dispense advice about animals are among the most environmentally sensitive beings in the world. Virtually everything they produce—from Tips on Holiday Safety to Tips on Traveling Safely with Your Dog—is made from recycled material. What goes around goes around again and again in the world of animal advice mavens, where, as in the physical world, matter is never destroyed but simply reappears in different configurations.

Because I travel frequently with my dogs—and because there was a deadline coming at me like a runaway eighteen-wheeler—I recently developed a keen interest in articles that set forth rules of the road for people who travel with their pets. After sampling enough items from this genre to become carsick (if not actually agoraphobic), I formulated a rule of my own: the more pedestrian the name of the fictitious dog or cat in a pet-travel article, the more pedestrian the article itself. A sterling example of this principle from the *Milwaukee Journal Sentinel* began like this: "Leaving Fido at home when you go on vacation isn't always an option."

I wasn't expecting lyricism from a writer whose idea of a snappy dog name is *Fido*, and I wasn't disappointed. "When traveling by car on a hot day, turn on the air conditioning if possible to keep the dog cool." Now why didn't I think of that? The next time I see a dog sailing down a highway with its head stuck out of a car window, I'll flag the driver down and suggest that he or she turn on the air conditioner.

After finishing "Travels with Fido," I read another pet-travel primer. This one began, "To Spot, the rattle of car keys is a magical sound." Spot's creator, who's probably acquainted with Fido's keeper, was eager to share the following discovery: "Barriers designed for station wagons or sport utility vehicles will confine a dog to the back." Whoa. Wait until I tell my brother-in-law *that*. He always refers to those contraptions as "doggie dicers."

The foregoing examples, like much of the advice contained in pet-travel articles, can be filed in the do-not-pour-steaming-hot-drinks-onto-your-crotch folder. Even more surprising, though, is the fact that people who write pet-travel articles are almost universally remiss in treating one critical topic. Granted, they'll all tell you to "take breaks at least every three hours to allow your pet to exercise and relieve itself," but they are resoundingly silent about the most critical piece of pet-travel information: how to find a suitable place to run your dogs. This knowledge is particularly important when you're whizzing along the highway and one of your dogs starts whimpering in a poignant manner, or when you arrive at your motel and discover that its lawn is the size of a card table.

"A place to run your dogs" is not synonymous with a "dog-walk area." Anyone smart enough not to pour steaming-hot drinks onto his or her lap can find a dog-walk area. The majority of rest stops have them, and many are even marked with big yellow signs for the benefit of those who forget to turn on the air conditioner in the car until the dog starts trying to break a window to stick his head out. A place to run your dogs, however, is as different from a dog-walk area as Pecorino Romano is from Cheez Whiz. Instead of the cabined, cribbed, all-dogs-must-be-walked-on-a-leash conformity that marks dog-walk areas, a place to run your dogs allows them to charge about with ears flapping and butts quivering as they investigate a whole new universe in which to leave their various scents. A place to run your dogs, in addition to giving them a chance to stretch out and express themselves on a larger canvas, allows you to enjoy them enjoying themselves, and that's one of the sweetest joys of owning a pug. Many a long and tedious trip has been lightened as a result of finding one or two ideal sites for running the dogs. The trick lies in

In the nick of time Fetch arrives to warn Harry that he's trapped on a rock.

knowing how to spot such locations, and that's one trick the pet-travel writers do not teach.

That omission is all the more puzzling because there are few places in the original forty-eight states that are farther than fifteen miles from a paved road, a McDonald's, or a place to run the dogs. Thus, you can begin to develop your run-finding skills right at home. Even if you live in one of those vertical coffins in what a lesser writer might refer to as a "concrete canyon," you're probably no more than a short drive from a place to run the dogs; but unlike a dog-walk area, a good running place isn't going to have a big yellow sign stuck in front. Indeed, most of the choice spots in which to run your dogs will have signs intended to throw you off the scent—signs that say things like Repeater Regional High School: Home of the Uzis, Cyberglitch Corporate Park, Temple of Mammon Mall, or the Mendenhall Inn. The reason these dog runs are coy about coming right out and saying "You and your eight dogs are welcome here" is simple: most of them don't want flocks of dogs scurrying about. Can you imagine that? But don't let this exclusionary attitude or the fact that your presence might legally constitute trespassing deter you.

The last place on the preceding list of dog runs—the Mendenhall Inn—is one that I discovered one autumn day as I was returning to my humble village in southeastern Pennsylvania. I had been to Hockessin, Delaware, about forty miles away, to visit my mother. I usually take two or three pugs along for company, and before I leave to return to my house, I let them run in the large field that abuts the nursing home where my mother lives.

As there were two people sitting on a bench near the field, I didn't want to risk having the dogs snuffling all over them. I decided, therefore, to look for another spot. My finely honed sense of dog-running places led me to pull into the parking lot next to the Mendenhall Inn, which is located a few miles north of the Delaware-Pennsylvania border. There I discovered that the parking lot is connected to a driveway which leads beyond the inn to another parking lot across from something called "The Grand Ballroom," which is probably used for wedding receptions, coming-out parties, and other joyous events.

The Grand Ballroom being deserted that afternoon, I parked the van and let the dogs out to run in a clearing in the adjacent woods. The afternoon was unusually warm for early November in these parts, and I welcomed the opportunity to rustle a few leaves while the dogs sniffed hither and yon. They were especially interested in three gigantic carved pumpkins that must have been dumped in the woods by druids after playing a decorative role in some recently concluded Halloween observance. After ten minutes of restorative solitude, the dogs and I were back in the van and on the way home.

Discoveries like the Mendenhall Inn are one of life's small but enduring joys. Had it not been for the need to air the dogs, I never would have had the chance to tarry in those woods and to muse over those pumpkins. The afternoon would have been the poorer for that loss.

We have made similar discoveries up and down the East Coast from Vermont to Georgia, and, it turns out, we have been discovered ourselves on occasion. The last time we stopped at the commodious field where raspberries grow wild next to a hotel in Phillipsburg, New Jersey, a young man came running out of the restaurant and said to my wife, "You're the people with the pugs. I was telling my girlfriend about you."

In closing, my fellow pug travelers, I suggest that you hit the road and begin developing your run-finding skills. Leave the leash-only parks to the more timid souls. There's something about strolling along in a place you've never seen, picking wild raspberries while your dogs race about exuberantly, that clears the mind and soothes the weary traveler's soul.

Chapter 21

As Lazy As Ludlum's Dog

In September 1998, somebody slipped a whoopee cushion under one of the most beloved legends in pug history. That somebody was Robert Hutchinson, who hid his fiendish device in a book he wrote entitled *For the Love of Pugs*. Any pug fanciers among Hutchinson's readers got the royal raspberry upon sitting down with his account of the night in 1572 that William the Silent's dog saved him from assassins.

Until Hutchinson came along, pug lovers had happily believed that the dog who saved William, the governor of the Netherlands, from certain death was a pug named Pompey. By barking, scratching, and finally jumping on the sleeping William's face, Pompey alerted his master to the danger lurking outside William's tent.

Although cynics occasionally grumbled that Pompey wasn't trying to save anybody's life—he merely wanted his breakfast early—pug fanciers believed the spunky little dog had changed the course of history, or at least William's life. In support of their belief, they pointed to the effigy of William in the cathedral at Delft. On this effigy there's a dog lying at William's feet, and pug fanciers have long claimed that the dog is a pug. Therefore, Pompey had to have been a pug.

Hutchinson, a research scientist at the American Museum of Natural History, claimed otherwise. To be precise, several Dutch dog fanciers with whom he spoke claimed otherwise. According to Hutchinson, they told him that the dog lying at William's feet in the effigy is a Kooikerhondje, a small white hound with bright orange markings.

What's more, Hutchinson reported, the dog's name wasn't Pompey, it was Kuntze. Hutchinson made this claim on the authority of Dutch historian Pieter Corneliszoon Hooft. In 1642, Hooft published *Nederlandse historien* in which he credited a Kooikerhondje named Kuntze with saving William's life.

Hutchinson's final proof in his brief against Pompey—cited for the benefit of those members of his audience who do not read seventeenth-century Dutch history books—is a biography of William the Silent that aired on Dutch television. In this Dutch-made program a Kooiker was cast in the role of William's canine savior.

Hutchinson's arguments appear to be airtight, but I am not one to let reality stand in the way of peace of mind. Consequently, upon reading those arguments, I resolved to travel to the Netherlands to confront the effigy of William at Delft, but on my way to the door I remembered I didn't have a passport. Besides, I don't like to travel farther than the nearest Borders—and that far only on a good day.

I wanted, nonetheless, to repair the damage done by Hutchinson's assault on the Pompey legend. If I couldn't dismantle the whoopee cushion, maybe I could give pug lovers something to make them proud. Surely one good myth deserves another, and even if the dog who changed the course of history in 1572 wasn't a pug, who's to say that pugs haven't changed the course of history in other ways? Or at least the course of our language?

Happily, it turns out, pugs have been responsible for many ripples in our linguistic stream. The oldest is the venerable expression "as lazy as Ludlam's dog."

Ludlam was a famous sorceress and hairdresser who put a hex on London Bridge in 1230 because the mayor of London, Richard Starkey, had set up tollbooths on the bridge. The tollbooths appeared shortly after a group of developers had convinced Starkey that a perfectly serviceable wooden bridge should be replaced by an ornate stone model. After hexing the bridge, Ludlum predicted it would either fall down soon or be moved to the middle of a great desert one day.

Some wags have suggested that a pug dog was on the other end of the line when E.T. phoned home.

Richard Starkey, who was suspected of taking kickbacks from the New London Bridge Authority, was incensed over Ludlum's hex, which he considered a sign of disrespect to him and his office. He conspired to have her drummed out of town. In order to escape the mayor's snare, Ludlum fled to the deepest woods. There she set up a beauty parlor in a cave. She called her shop The Rape of the Lock, a title that Alexander Pope (1688–744) used for his poem of the same name.

Ludlum took her pug, Sanford, with her into exile. Because Ludlum was paranoid, she wouldn't tell anyone Sanford's name, so people referred to him as "Ludlum's Dog" when they began telling stories about his legendary laziness. This was a dog who leaned against the wall of Ludlum's cave when he barked, which wasn't often. Ludlum, who was a trifle hard of hearing, lost a lot of business because Sanford failed to alert her when people came by to get a reading or a haircut. After word of Sanford's laziness had drifted back to London, townspeople began using the expression "as lazy as Ludlum's dog" to describe their least-industrious brethren.

English being the mother of our language, we shouldn't be surprised that English pugs were responsible for other linguistic enhancements. Let us consider one more, the harrowing expression "Let slip the dogs of war."

Warren's pugs also inspired the expression "Call off the dogs…"

In the fifteenth century an old hayseed named Warren, who lived in the English village of Muttonchops, had a trio of manic pugs, each one wilder than the next. Villagers in Muttonchops referred to these pugs collectively as *The Dogs of Warren*, but their real names were Huey, Dewey, and Louie.

The Dogs of Warren got into a lot of bother. They especially liked to tip over outhouses, which were made of dried straw in those days. Warren's friends thought this was hilarious. Whenever they'd see somebody nip out to the loo, they'd holler, "Let slip the dogs of Warren," which eventually was shortened to the expression we know today. (Warren's pugs also inspired the expression "Call off the dogs," which is what the unfortunate bloke in the outhouse usually hollered.)

Some of the expressions for which pugs are responsible have been brought into English from other languages. Chief among these is the expression "Hungry dogs will eat dirty pudding," which was inspired by an Italian pug's heroic appetite. In nineteenth-century Italy, a pug named Gucci was fond of the wine the Vicar Arlotto used in saying Mass. Arlotto, who said Mass quite often, kept a cask of wine in the back of the church, and Gucci figured out that by licking the spigot he could have a drink whenever he fancied one.

As Gucci consumed more and more wine, he became fearful of getting caught. Whenever Arlotto called him, Gucci ran away. One day he ran so far that he couldn't find his way home.

Left to his own devices, Gucci started hanging around the dumpster behind an espresso bar in Milan. One day the head waiter threw away a batch of tiramisu that had been dropped on the floor. Gucci found the tiramisu in the trash and set upon the pudding at once. A gaggle of fashion designers who were passing by noticed this. One of them stopped and exclaimed, "Will you look at that! Hungry dogs will eat dirty pudding."

The preceding examples culled from the many contributions pugs have made to our language should help pug fanciers to forget Robert Hutchinson's sacking of Pompey. If there are any pug lovers still longing for proof that a pug changed the course of history, they should long no longer. A pug named IBM is believed to have invented the punch cards that ran the earliest computers.

IBM belonged to an American engineer named Herman Hollerith. In 1880, the twenty-year-old Hollerith went to work for the census bureau. In those days census-takers wrote the names and ages of every person in

> *A pug named IBM is believed to have invented the punch cards that ran the earliest computers.*

every household in the United States on individual cards, one card per household. Naturally, it took a long time to add up all the information on those cards.

One day IBM got hold of one of Hollerith's cards and began chewing on it. When Hollerith saw the card, he freaked. "The dog's eating my homework!" he yelled. Then he realized that the number of holes in the card, twenty-one, equaled the number of people living in the house the card represented. This gave him the idea of putting holes in the cards instead of numbers. Then he developed a hand-fed press that read and tabulated the holes in the cards. Hollerith's system was the forerunner of today's computers. It proved so fast that data from the 1890 Census was tabulated in only two years, saving the government $5 million and several years' time.

Buoyed by his success, Hollerith founded the Tabulating Machine Company in 1896. This later became the Computer Tabulating Recording Company, which in 1924 changed its name to International Business Machines—IBM for short—in honor of Hollerith's dog.

Because people have always asked what the letters in IBM's name stood for originally, I put that question to an historian at IBM headquarters recently.

"It's Beyond Me," the historian replied.

"Do you mean to say you don't know what the initials stood for?" I responded.

"No," said the historian. "I mean to say the dog's name was 'It's Beyond Me,' or 'IBM' for short."

Chapter 22
Dexter

The best thing to do with good advice is to ignore it. Ever since fifth grade—a mere half century ago—I have hewn unflinchingly to this belief, studiously ignoring the advice of parents, teachers, physicians, friends, warning labels, no-trespassing signs, speed limits, weathermen, operating instructions, and owner's manuals. I make an especial point of ignoring the advice I extend to others, particularly the advice I put in writing. That is how I came to be in possession of Dexter and Fetch, two enormously charming pug boys.

On the last Friday in June 1999, I spent the hours from midnight to 10:30 A.M. writing. After a brief nap I checked the answering machine and found a message from my wife Mary Ann, who had called from work to say that a one-year-old male pug had been surrendered recently at a shelter in Philadelphia. Was there anyone I could think of who might be interested in the lad?

I called Mary Ann at once to say that I did, indeed, know someone who was interested in the dog. The manic chuckle that accompanied my announcement was as good as an elbow in the ribs. She realized to her dismay that the person to whom I was referring and the person to whom she was speaking were one and the same. She replied in the extra-patient tone she reserves for my more impulsive schemes that she didn't think we needed a seventh dog at the moment. Besides, she had already told two people at work who had previously expressed an interest in pugs that there was now one available.

I phoned the shelter anyway and learned that if no one spoke up on the dog's behalf, he would be put up for adoption soon. I explained that my wife had told some friends of hers about the dog, but if they didn't call by the end of the day, I'd take him.

The sudden, unilateral decision to acquire a dog, especially when made by a person recently emerged from a nap, violates the advice that I and other "experts" give to prospective dog owners. Nevertheless, because of writer's intuition or pug owner's intuition or both, I knew this dog would be special. He had to be. He was a pug. He'd surely fit in with our clan and bring his own special seasoning to the mix.

Two days later we drove fifty miles to the shelter in Philadelphia to meet the young, unneutered Dexter. He was in a small crate in the grooming room, having just been bathed, and was barking madly at a schnauzer in a crate across the way. When the director of adoptions opened Dexter's crate and attached a leash to his collar, he dragged her over to the schnauzer's crate, put his front end down, his back end up, and barked out an invitation to play, stopping only long enough to deposit a small lake beside the schnauzer's crate.

We didn't want to interrupt Dexter's fun, but we *had* driven more than an hour to make his acquaintance; and we wanted to have a closer look at him, not only because he was such a spirited fellow but also because he was the oddest-looking pug we had ever seen. He looked nothing like our pugs. Less than nothing, in fact. Where they are short and squat, he is tall and rangy. Where they have troll-like faces with skin rolls that form canopies over their noses, he has a face like a boxer's—no nose roll at all and a beak as plain as the nose on your face. Where they have bodies that resemble velour-covered sausages, he sports a tuck-up worthy of a whippet. Where they have no dewclaws, he does.

I gazed in awe at Dexter, wondering where I had seen his like before. Then I remembered. He looked like one of those pugs on the hundred-year-old postcards you find at flea markets or pug owners' houses. In fact, we have one of those postcards framed on a bedroom wall.

Having violated the precept against choosing a dog with all deliberate speed, I hastened to violate the commandment about

Dexter is that rare pug capable of catching food with his mouth instead of his forehead.

waiting to bring a new dog home until you have lots of time to spend with him. Dexter was neutered at the shelter the following day, an operation that required more surgery than usual because the vet had to go poking around in Dexter's abdominal cavity in search of an undescended testicle. We picked Dexter up on Tuesday, and on Wednesday we left to visit to my wife's parents at their summer place in western Massachusetts. Dexter was given little more than half a day to make the acquaintance of our other six pugs and to look around at his new digs, the second new locale he had seen recently, before setting off on a six-hour trip with his new roommates to another place with which they were familiar but he was not.

Dex weathered it all with aplomb. Actually, he moved in and took over. No one had attempted to breed our three spayed females in some time, and one or two of them seemed flattered by his attentions at first. Our boys, with whom he also tried to mate, did not look pleased. They looked, instead, as if they had died and gone to prison.

When we arrived at the lakeside cottage in Massachusetts, the hulking Lab-like dog that lived in the cottage next door came ambling over to investigate. Patty, the alpha dog in our crew at that time, charged at the visitor, who was nearly four times Patty's size, and ran her off. When the dog was back on her own lawn, she turned to face Patty. Dexter immediately charged to Patty's aid, barking furiously. The other pugs, meanwhile, were busy looking for a white flag and a pole on which to fly it.

On Saturday, a mere four days after we had collected Dex, he attended a family birthday celebration at which there were fifteen people and a like number of dogs, including several Jack Russells and Labrador retrievers. None of this fazed him: he was cooler than the other side of the pillow. In fact, by the way he behaved, you'd have thought it was his party. He was the perfect maître d', charming and attentive to all, no matter what they were eating. He also revealed an impressive talent for catching treats in midair that far exceeded the ordinary pug's ability. Our pugs usually catch things with their foreheads.

Dexter even found time to start the party's only fight. At some point in the afternoon we heard raucous barking from the dock next door. When we looked up to see what the hullabaloo was about, there came Dexter, coat dripping, racing across the lawn with half a dozen of the neighbors' dogs in furious pursuit. The chase reminded me of the villagers running Frankenstein out of town. Dex had apparently invited himself swimming with some of the other dogs, and they had taken offense when he couldn't produce a swim-club membership card. After he had reached his own yard, Dexter leaped onto the bench of the picnic table to escape his pursuers. If he hadn't put on the brakes at the last minute, he would have left skid marks on a plate full of quiche, two lovely cakes, and other comestibles.

A while later, after peace had broken out, Dexter spotted one of his adversaries and was off like a shot. Unfortunately, I was sitting in a rickety chair on a slight incline holding Dexter's lead at the time. I went crashing into the empty chair next to me and then to the ground. The first thing I saw when I stopped laughing was Dexter's long blue lead, looking like the tail on a dog-shaped kite, making its way across the lawn.

We managed to survive the rest of the weekend without major incident, returning home in the early hours of July 5. The following day the shelter in Philadelphia called again. "You won't believe this…," the woman began.

Once more I gleefully neglected my own advice, and thus commenced the story of Fetch, a tale we take up in the following chapter.

Chapter 23
Fetch

An open letter to Fetch's former owner(s).

Dear Sir(s) and/or Madam(s):

As near as I can tell, Fetch has been gone a hundred days. I expect you must be missing him by now, so I thought I'd let you know what has become of your former dog.

We adopted Fetch on Wednesday, July 7, after the dog catcher in Philadelphia had picked him up for vagrancy a week or so before. The folks at the shelter where Fetch was then staying had no idea how long he had been at large, nor did they know what his name might be or whom they should call to say he had been found, as he wasn't wearing an ID tag. Consequently, when you didn't phone to inquire about him, Fetch was put up for adoption.

As my wife and I were taking Fetch home that broiling summer day, we talked about possible names for him and wondered what you had called him. Were you the kind of owner who agonizes over a dog's name before you get the dog? Or did you allow his name to evolve out of the warp and woof of existence? It's been our experience that agonizers have dogs named Dot Matrix or Don Sequitur or something impossibly clever. The warp and woofers have dogs that answer to things like Trashmaster or Whatshisface. We're certified warp and woofers—in dogs and in many other regards—and that's how Fetch got his new name, but I'm getting ahead of the tale.

The thing that struck me as we were wondering what to call this fawn-colored pug stranger was the fact that he would never hear his "real" name again. I tried to imagine how odd that would feel. One's name is one's dearest possession, the sweetest sound in the world, it is said; and your youngster—the shelter figured he was less than a year old—would never hear that sound again, to "revel in his authenticity" as the psychobabblers might say, unless, of course, you had named him one of those expletives I scream at the computer whenever I get disconnected while downloading an especially large MP3 file.

Anyway, after we'd taken Fetch home, he managed the introductions to our seven other pugs adroitly. Six of those dogs, ranging in age from not quite three to a little past seven at the time, were born in our house; the other one, just slightly older than Fetch, had been adopted eight days earlier from the same shelter. We told the good folks at the shelter that if they were going to insist on ringing us up whenever a stray or surrendered pug came in, we were going to have to resort to caller ID.

At the first supper Fetch revealed a certain manic eagerness about food. We wondered if he had always been that way or if his time on the street, however long that might have been, was the reason he began barking madly and whirling about like a dervish before running and hurling himself against the door between the kitchen and the sun porch. Dogs, like football players, have their individual ways of getting up for a game; but Fetch's, by far, is the most distinctive we have witnessed. The other dogs, who generally sit around discussing current events politely as I fix their meals, looked at Fetch as if he were barmy.

After several days we were still looking for something more personal than "Hey, Little Guy" to call Fetch. Then he solved that problem for us. One night as I was eating dinner, I felt something crash into my right leg. It was Fetch, with a squeaky toy in his mouth and a gleam in his eye. I took the toy, wincing at its sogginess, and tossed it across the kitchen. Fetch bounded after it, seized it, and raced back with it. Did you teach him that? It's an endearing routine. Mealtimes mustn't be the same without it.

Thinking he has eluded his pursuers, Fetch peers out from his hiding place behind the pole.

I especially enjoy Fetch's jubilant return with the toy. Like everything else about him, his technique is a few degrees short of plumb, a result of the lavish energy he brings to most endeavors. Because Fetch usually mistimes his leap when he's racing back with his catch—always taking off too soon—he's on the down slope by the time he arrives. He gets this man-overboard look in his eyes as he reaches out with his front paws to get a purchase on my leg.

So that's how Fetch got his name. My wife wasn't fond of it, but it fits, and he wears it well. Indeed, he recognizes it now; and if he prefers his former name, he's been too polite to say anything about it. Whether he prefers his former home, we'll never know. We haven't seen him whining at the door, and he's never tried to run away or to slip a note to the FedEx man, so we assume he's happy here. Because he was a little restless his first night, we bumped one of the other dogs whose turn it was to sleep in bed with us—we use a four-on-four-off bed rotation—so Fetch wouldn't feel lonely sleeping in the kitchen with three of his new friends. He kept jumping out of bed to go exploring, and we had to put him in a crate. He settled down at once, so we thought he was used to sleeping in a crate, not a bed; but he's cottoned to the bed in the meantime, and when it's not his turn to sleep with us, he camps out in the kitchen with the other dogs.

Fetch enjoys riding in the van, and he puts his own hyperkinetic spin on that activity, too, standing with his front paws on the back of the rear seat and barking at the vehicle behind us. We always get a chuckle out of this, and sometimes when I look in the rearview mirror, I see the people in the car behind us laughing, too. If we ever get kamikazed from behind, I'll know why.

I don't want to take up too much of your time, and I suspect this may be painful for you. In fact, I hesitated to write for that reason, but I thought you might take some comfort in knowing that Fetch was OK and happily employed keeping the world safe from tailgaters. I do want to ask you one more thing though. Were you in the habit of breaking the second commandment?

The other morning I was playing fetch with Fetch and chiding him gently about a few accidents he he'd had in the house recently. As he was dashing across the kitchen to retrieve his toy, I said in my best Jimmy Swaggert voice, "You must learn to reNOUNCE your sinfulness and to acCEPT Jesus Christ into your life."

At the sound of "Jesus Christ," Fetch stopped in his tracks, turned his head, and gave me the oddest look. I figured you might have used the Lord's name in correcting Fetch. Either that or I had stumbled on his previous name. I'm not being critical, mind you. For the longest time our dog Hans thought his name was "goddamn it, Hans."

Well, I guess that's all I have to say for now. If you have or acquire other dogs, I hope things work out better with them. Meanwhile, Fetch sends his best and says not to worry. Everything's cool with him.

Chapter 24

Food for Thought

Some of my best ideas have presented themselves while I was gazing idly at my dogs with my mind in neutral, which is one of its two favorite gears, the other being "park." In September 2001, while my wife and I and were on vacation, I enjoyed such a moment of inspired divine neutrality. Actually, I have been on vacation since 1979—which was twenty-four years ago if anyone's counting. I do a little writing and the occasional web-design project only to prevent all that leisure time from becoming oppressive.

During this particular segment of my ongoing vacation, we traveled with our six pugs to the Berkshire Mountains in western Massachusetts, where my wife's family owned a cottage that over-looks a lake. The eight of us had the cottage and the surrounding woods to ourselves. There wasn't a neighbor in residence within a quarter mile, and the nearest paved road was forty yards or so up a hillside. If you've seen *On Golden Pond*, you know the kind of scene I'm talking about. Ordinarily a deluxe eight-nights-and-seven-days vacation package like this is not available free of cost unless you're willing to fly to some godforsaken place and spend several hours in an uncomfortable folding chair while someone tries to bully you and a bunch of other freeloaders into buying time-shares in a condominium.

One Golden-Pond dusk I was reclining in a lounge chair set to the laid-back position, holding a jar of macadamia nuts and gazing at the dogs, who were occupying their bed and the other two chairs in the room as well. I tried to open the jar surreptitiously, but pugs can hear any kind of food receptacle—bag, jar, can, box, pouch, sack, or freezer-proof Ziplock® container—being opened within a hundred-yard radius, even if they're asleep and an ancient, black-and-white, three-channel television set is playing nearby. No sooner had I given the lid of the jar a slow, stealthy twist than the dogs leaped into the full-awake position and converged on my chair like a pack of wolves eyeing a three-legged kitten up a tree. For the next several minutes I doled out macadamia nuts in a one-for-you-two-for-me ratio. All told, I went through $42 worth of Hawaii's finest. I came away from the experience not only with my all fingers intact but also with an idea that will revolutionize the dog-food industry. Before I reveal that idea, however, a little history lesson is in order.

Dog food is one of those happy developments that has, unhappily, changed little since it was invented. Both dog food and a primitive form of typewriter first appeared in 1860, yet typewriters have progressed much further than dog food has in the meantime. Typewriters have become sleek and streamlined; they've developed a memory and learned to spell better than we humans can. Dog food, on the other hand, still looks like the dog's breakfast; and judging by the way our pugs take a lively interest in whatever we're eating, may taste something like it, too.

Credit for the invention of dog food goes to James Spratt, an electrician from Cincinnati, Ohio. Spratt sailed to London in 1860, hoping to sell lightning rods to a population well acquainted with bad weather. When his ship reached land, he noticed a pack of dogs scavenging for discarded ships' biscuits on the quayside, a whimsical British word for *dock*. As Spratt gazed idly at the dogs, lightning struck.

"Egad," he thought, "that [stuff] they're fighting over isn't fit for a dog. I should be selling dog food instead of these stodgy old lightning rods."

Spratt did not make this determination hastily, nor was he a mere flash in the pantheon of the lightning rod set. By 1860, he already held three patents: one for improvement in the alloys contained in the points of lightning rods, one for improvement in the

Sadly the members of the food kitchen were a few sandwiches short of a picnic when they met for their weekly test session.

attachments for lightning conductors, and one for general improvement in lightning rod design.

Spratt's dog food—a blend of wheat meal, vegetables, beetroot, and meat—wasn't 100 percent complete and balanced nutrition for all stages of a dog's life, nor was it tested in feed trials conducted in accordance with anybody's protocols; but dogs fell on it as though it was the greatest thing prior to sliced bread, which wouldn't be invented for another sixty-eight years. Therefore, Spratt set up shop in Holborn, London, where he began to manufacture "dog cakes."

One of Spratt's employees was Charles Cruft, who signed on with the dog-cake company as an office boy in 1876, immediately after graduating from college. Cruft, who turned down a job in his family's jewelry business to go to work for Spratt, eventually became a dog-cake salesman. He is best remembered, however, for starting the Crufts Dog Show in 1891, a production that not only made him wealthy but also came to be known as the greatest dog show in the world. Nice work for a chap who allegedly preferred the company of cats.

Although Spratt and Cruft have long since gone to their eternal rewards, the list of ingredients in dog food is little different today than it was in their time. Science has improved the diet by adding vitamins, dyes, minerals, and preservatives; but the ingredients from the primary dog food groups—meat, grain, and vegetables—remain virtually unchanged.

My experience with macadamia nuts and other foods I enjoy convinces me that dog food manufacturers have seriously neglected canine taste buds. Even those products sold as "gourmet" dog foods are thoroughly pedestrian. Their flavors are designed to replicate barbecue sauce, cheese, tacos, French fries, peanut butter, pepperoni, liver, and such. Would you call those kinds of foods gourmet? I certainly wouldn't, and neither would any self-respecting pug. Pugs know the difference between diner food and fine dining. They'll make a fuss over peanut butter, but they'd prefer macadamia nuts. They'll settle for lamb parts and rice, but they'd rather have rack of lamb and risotto. They'll eat grains, but they'd sooner eat granola with organically grown blueberries. These and other preferences have been verified time and again in our test kitchen.

Anyone who has read or written a few dog-care books (actually, I've written more than I've read) knows that with the exception of sight and restraint, a dog's senses are generally superior to a human's. Yet we persist in feeding our dogs as though they possessed three olfactory nerves and monaural taste buds. Dogs, meanwhile, long to eat in surround sound. Thus, we should feed our pugs the things they really want to eat, and they, in turn, should leave us in peace when we, too, are trying to enjoy the things we really want to eat.

If I wished to take time from my busy vacation schedule, I could cook up some true gourmet dog food, make a fortune, and retire to the Berkshires. I would prefer instead to watch others do the work, so I'll content myself with passing on the aforementioned ideas for new dog food flavors to people more ambitious than I. In the meantime I'll patiently await the day when I'm strolling through the dog food aisle in the supermarket with my mind in neutral and discover a bag of dog food labeled "Kibbles 'n' Macadamia Nutz" or "Carpaccio of Ostrich With White Truffle Oil Snacks for Dogs." My dogs and I stand ready to celebrate that glorious occasion.

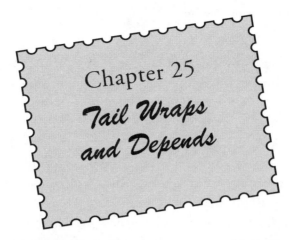

Chapter 25

Tail Wraps and Depends

My fifty-eighth birthday party was a memorable affair, I'm told. Though I don't remember too much about it, I do recall a flagon of neon-orange Mogen David 20/20, which not a single guest would join me in drinking, and our pug dog Hans, equally surreal-looking in a black harness, tail wrap, and Depends. As Keith Richards once said in a similar context, "You shoulda been there."

That Hans was able to attend this bacchanal was the second-best present any major dude could have asked for on his birthday. Four months earlier a degenerating nerve disease had left Hans with the mobility and general prospects of a harp seal facing a mob of hunters, yet there he was on the second Saturday night of January 2001 making his ungainly but fashionable way among the guests, dodging spilled drinks and diving on spilled food right along with our other five pugs. At the risk of having my curmudgeon's license revoked, I must confess that the sight of Hans brought a tear to my eye—and not solely because I hate to see good food and drink being spilled.

I have been partial to Hans since shortly after the day he was born—a bitter December 30, 1993. Hans was one of six puppies, a large brood by pug standards and an unforgettable bunch by any measure. Eight days after Hans and his mates had come squiggling into the world, an ice storm shut down southeastern Pennsylvania. Before the ice could get a chance to fade away graciously, one snowstorm after another—and an additional ice storm or two—visited the region, closing schools, delaying buses, and disrupting bingo and ham-supper schedules. As a result Hans and his mates were housebound until St. Patrick's day, nearly a month past the time when new puppies should have begun to sample the glories of the outdoors, however briefly. Talk about puppies being raised underfoot! This bunch was raised under our skins.

About the time puppies open their eyes and begin to develop facial characteristics, Hans took on an unfortunate resemblance to Jack Elam. That, of course, is something of a redundancy because there's no fortunate resemblance to Mr. Elam, as anyone who has seen one of his ninety-seven films can attest.

Hans' large, wandering eyes, which allowed him to see even farther around a corner than Mr. Elam could in his prime, were complemented by a large, protruding belly and a truculent, self-important expression. This singular appearance was matched by a singular personality. Hans, to put it bluntly, could be obnoxious. Soon after he had discovered he could bark, he began to yelp at four o'clock each morning, a grating, imperious sound that invariably set his five litter mates to screeching also. The racket would not subside until my wife or I went shuffling over to the puppies' crate in response to their ultimatum. Yet no matter how annoyed I was at being pushed around by this tiny dictator and his lieutenants, I couldn't help smiling—after my second cup of coffee—at the thought of Hans hopping up and down in a fresh puddle, eyes casting about like rogue searchlights, a look of twisted indignation on his Jack Elam face. Thus began most mornings in the winter of 1993-94.

The older Hans got, the more keenly he followed the dictates of his own drummer, whom I took to be the ghost of Keith Moon. No sooner was Hans able to run than he began greeting my wife's returns from work by hurling himself against the kitchen door, causing it to rattle most perturbingly. When we took the puppies for walks, Hans was always the first to head off on his own and the last to heed our summonses to return.

Hans' failures in comportment, coupled with certain deficiencies in conformation, made him a less-than-ideal candidate for showing, but we decided to keep him anyway. Indeed, we forked over $1,000 for that privilege to the people for whom we had whelped and raised the litter of which Hans was such a noticeable part. That decision, if you must know, was largely mine. I'd come up short often enough in comportment to appreciate a fellow traveler when I saw one, even when he was putting his foot through the screen door on the front porch in his haste to get outside. Moreover, the evaluation given me once by the principal of the school where I taught—"Despite a charming exterior, he tends to do exactly as he pleases"—fit Hans like a detention slip. But so what? Isn't doing exactly what you please the point of life? The main trouble with being a dog is having to do what somebody else pleases most of the time.

Another trouble with being a dog—and with being human too—is having to do as nature pleases. This lesson was rammed home to Hans and me in the summer of 2000. Our education began in June when Hans' jaunty walk went a little wobbly around the edges. He sometimes hesitated, as though he were doing a cost-benefit analysis, before jumping into the van, and he no longer hit the kitchen door with his usual impact. Our vet, suggesting that Hans was becoming a tad arthritic, prescribed Glyco-Flex, which is commonly given to dogs with joint problems. When that didn't help—Hans was beginning to scramble into the van instead of hurtling upward with his usual projectile force—the vet, who couldn't find anything structurally wrong with Hans, recommended that we take him to a neurosurgeon who practiced at a specialty clinic about an hour's drive away.

We had taken other dogs to that clinic, and the only good thing about those visits was the road we took to get there, which winds through Valley Forge State Park, a lovely and tranquil preserve. The rest of the trip is a cold, hungry winter any time of year.

Hans' first visit was no exception. X-rays revealed a slight scoliosis just behind Hans' shoulder blades. The vet thought this might be the cause of Hans' increasingly faltering gait. Hans, for his part, thought the whole episode was a fine chance for people to make his acquaintance. When the vet left the examination room to see if the X-ray facilities were available, Hans fairly sprinted through the doorway after him as though he (Hans) had just been reunited with his birth father.

While we were pondering the next step for Hans, nature came calling again, and I wound up in the hospital for thirteen days and two surgical procedures: the first to remove one hundred ml of fluid from around my heart, the second to remove two liters of fluid from around my lungs. Medical science has yet to determine what was wrong with me, a failure shared with the former principal who had given me the bad, albeit truthful, evaluation; but after I had been released from the hospital, I no longer made sloshing sounds when I walked, and I was able to cover more than fifteen or twenty paces without having to stop for breath.

When I returned home from the hospital in mid-August, it was obvious that something was wrong with Hans. He wobbled terribly when he walked, and he was no longer able to leap onto the couch. Instead of spending my first night home in quiet celebration, surrounded by all the foods I wasn't allowed to have in hospital, I spent the night holding my little miscreant of a dog and wondering what the hell was going to go wrong next.

The following week we made our way through Valley Forge State Park to the neurosurgeon's once again. This time Hans had a myelogram, an examination in which a dye that is visible on X rays is injected into the fluid-filled space around the spinal cord. The myelogram, in addition to setting us back $1,100, produced an adverse affect on Hans' mobility—without producing a diagnosis.

To add irony to insult, after we had been told that the results from the myelogram were inconclusive, we were informed that for another $1,100 Hans could have an MRI (Magnetic Resonance Imaging) exam. This procedure *might* pinpoint the source of Hans' trouble, but even so, a spinal operation in the area where that trouble most likely resided—somewhere near his shoulder blades— promised little chance of success, so little that the neurosurgeon was loath to risk it at any price.

Medical maintenance, the neurosurgeon reported, was our best bet, so Hans began receiving ten milligrams of Prednisone daily.

Prednisone is a corticosteroid known for its anti-inflammatory effects. If we had wanted Hans to develop a wretched thirst, to redistribute his weight until he looked like an overbred dairy goat, and to urinate at the slightest stimulation—outdoors or in—the prednisone could have been counted a success. Unfortunately, we had hoped it would enable him to walk a little better.

Stuck between a rock and a wet spot, we watched Hans grow worse. Not only did he walk with increasing difficulty, but also, when he lay down, his hind legs splayed out at grotesque angles so that he looked as if he had just fallen out of a tenth-floor window. Hope as we might for a sudden reversal of misfortune, we finally had to admit that we were faced with two miserly choices: a doggie cart or an operation that was all but certain to fail.

I rejected the first option out of hand. No doggie cart yet devised is large enough to hold that dog's spirit, and I was damned if I was going to consign him to spend the rest of his life as a wind-up toy.

The second option—an MRI followed by surgery—was equally distasteful. As there's nothing that will shake your faith in conventional veterinary medicine quicker than spending $1,100 on a diagnostic procedure that doesn't yield a diagnosis and has an adverse effect on your dog, I began to consider alternate therapies for Hans. Being something of a control freak who hates to admit failure in any arena, I was determined that Hans was going to walk better—perhaps not normally (I'm also something of a realist), but for sure he was going to do a damn sight better than he had been doing.

I began to wean Hans off that vile prednisone, and I took him to an acupuncturist who also performed veterinary orthopedic manipulation on problem dogs. This vet seemed more enthusiastic about the quality of Hans' X-rays than the prospects for his improvement. I also found it odd that the vet didn't allow dogs' owners to witness the acupuncture sessions because "they tend to get freaked out by the needles." I didn't bother to ask whether the vet was referring to the dogs or their owners. I merely sat in the waiting room paging through out-of-date magazines and hoping for the best.

The best this vet could do wasn't good enough. Hans was now beginning to lose control of his bladder and bowels. The vet said this wasn't a promising sign. When I talked to him on the phone on the last Friday of September 2000, I asked if there were other treatments we could try.

"Magnets, faith healers, anything, even if it smacks of quackery." Those were my exact words.

"I sometimes think that what I do (with acupuncture) smacks of quackery" was the vet's exact reply.

As I was mulling that one over later in the evening, I received a phone call from my wife, whose car had broken down about three hours north of us on a trip to New England. I didn't want to leave Hans at home unattended for six hours while I went to pick up my wife, so I decided to take him and another dog with me. They charged down the two steps from the side porch to the driveway, and Hans, as was his custom then, went hurrying off in the wrong direction, hoping to score a crab apple for the journey.

Perhaps "hurrying" isn't the best word to describe Hans' progress. He tumbled down the steps before I could pick him up, and even though his hind legs locked crosswise behind him in a way they had never done before, he dragged himself toward the crab apple tree. By the time I got to him, the tops of his hind feet were bleeding. His zest for life, which had always been one of his most endearing traits, was obviously going to be a problem in his reduced circumstances.

By early October Hans was on his last legs—his front ones. His inability to walk meant that he had to be carried outdoors, and carefully at that, because any sort of excitement was enough to set off his hair-trigger bladder. As those excitements included being fed, hearing the doorbell ring, being picked up, and a host of other stimuli, we kept a stack of towels and a clean pet bed at the ready in the kitchen, where, thankfully, the floor was covered with sturdy linoleum. My wife washed the pet bed at least once, sometimes more, each day; and I spent a lot of time on my knees, grumbling as I wiped up yet another puddle.

As slim as the chances were that spinal surgery would do Hans any good, it was beginning to look like our best option. We were about to sign him up for that crapshoot when I called our regular vet to tell her about the failed acupuncture treatments. She replied patiently, as she often does to many things I say, that I should have taken Hans to one Judith Shoemaker, D.V.M., "who *knows* acupuncture."

I called Shoemaker's office promptly and was told that the earliest she could see Hans was the first week in December. I could, however, have a telephone consultation sooner if I wanted. The next afternoon at four I talked on the phone with Shoemaker for nearly fifty minutes while she was en route from someplace to another in her car. She said she would try to see Hans before December if she got a break in her schedule. In the meantime I should find something called A.C.A. Joint Supplement and mix one-quarter of a teaspoon in with each of his meals, gradually increasing the dose until he was receiving a full teaspoon daily.

The conversation with Shoemaker was encouraging. Her intelligence was obvious, her confidence and enthusiasm infectious, and there was a take-charge attitude about her that appealed to me. I set about at once trying to locate A.C.A. Joint Supplement.

Neither our regular vet nor the Internet were any help in that regard, so I saddled up the van and drove thirty-four miles to Shoemaker's office. Located on a country road just above the Mason-Dixon Line in southeastern Pennsylvania, this office is unlike any other veterinarian's place I have ever seen. To begin with, it's situated on the grounds of the Mobile Mansion Mart, a complex that includes a nondescript, single-story, brick-and-cinder-block building surrounded by several mobile mansions, which look suspiciously like double-wide trailers.

One door in the single-story building leads to the sales office of the Mobile Mansion Mart. Another door bears a sign that reads "Equine Services." Behind that door is a singular office roughly two hundred feet wide and fifty feet deep. There's a long desk immediately inside the door and a shorter desk perpendicular to that one on its right. Twenty feet or so behind the desks are two horse stalls. To the right of the desks is the examination area. There are no tiny rooms, steel tables, or faintly unnerving antiseptic smells here, though you will find the occasional candle burning. In place of the customary fire hall furniture and robust linoleum floor found in most vets' offices are a dozen oriental carpets of varying sizes and patterns, a number of interesting wall hangings, two sofas and several upholstered chairs arranged in conversation areas, two small desks, and a few bookcases.

"This," I thought, "is what a vet's office would look like if the sixties hadn't been trampled underfoot by fear, suspicion, and linear thinking." Of course, a lot of things would be better if the sixties hadn't been trampled underfoot. The times may have been a-changin' back then, but they've changed for the worse in the meantime.

Two days after Hans had begun taking the A.C.A. Joint Supplement, he ventured a few steps on his own. They were shaky, but they were steps in the right direction. As unsteady as he was on his feet—and despite the fact that he still dragged himself along most of the time—this was the best news I had received since the home-care people who had been coming around to stick me in the butt with an antibiotic every day for the first five weeks after I'd been discharged from the hospital announced that one of my doctors had told them they wouldn't need to be visiting anymore. For this I was grateful from the bottom of my bottom.

"[Shoot]," I thought. "If this vet can get Hans on his feet a little bit this quickly—without even laying eyes on him—I can't wait to see what she does in person."

Hans' first visit to Shoemaker was even more encouraging. The examination began on the floor on a rubber runner between the desks and the horse stalls. While she manipulated Hans' spine, Shoemaker explained that the conformation mandated by the AKC standard leaves pugs prone to hemivertebrae, ruptured disks, and other spinal problems. Indeed, Hans' X-rays indicated that he has a few deformed vertebrae in addition to a slight scoliosis. These

Like the Buddha, Hans has always believed the attainment of nirvana was possible in this life.

conditions, which may have been present from birth, could have been aggravated by some sort of neck injury.

What's more, Hans' scoliosis was adversely affected by compensatory hypermobility, which strains and puts pressure on the spinal cord. The outer layer of the cord tells a dog where his legs are. The bottom portion tells a dog's legs what to do. Neither of these messages was getting through to Hans' hind legs. Nor were his bowels and bladder in communication with the controlling spinal authorities. By manipulating Hans' spine, Shoemaker sought to prevent the hypermobility from further stimulating his body to lay down more bone, which would further compress his spinal column and nerves.

When Shoemaker had finished manipulating Hans' spine, she exclaimed that his neck was probably two inches longer than it had been when he arrived. Hans, for his part, smiled and shook himself vigorously.

Next came the acupuncture portion of the visit. Shoemaker's goal in that procedure was to stimulate the nerve endings in areas that feed back to the portion of the spine affected by Hans's structural problems. As she placed tiny needles into various places on Hans's person, Shoemaker called out the names of the insertion points to her assistant Donna, who recorded them. Shoemaker further explained that acupuncture attempts to stimulate duplicate wiring in the nervous system. By stimulating what is working, acupuncture can sometimes stimulate what's not.

After Hans had spent about ten minutes sitting on the floor next to Shoemaker with needles sticking out of him, the veterinarian announced that if Hans' nails were shorter, they wouldn't compromise his walking. With that she carried him to a wing chair. Sitting in the chair with Hans on her left and her left arm forming a safety bar in front of him, Shoemaker deftly performed a ritual that normally takes my wife and me twice as long to do. Hans merely continued smiling.

Just when I thought there were no further wonders to behold, Shoemaker outfitted Hans with a tail wrap, an ingenious device that begins at the base of a dog's tail and extends that tail by a factor of two or three—perhaps four in Hans' case. The wrap, which is fashioned from an Ace bandage and features a loop at its tip, is used for tail-walking a dog. Tail-walking consists of holding a dog by the loop at the end of his wrapped tail, lifting him gently to his feet, then maintaining slight pressure and a forty-five-degree angle as you follow him along. The purpose of this exercise, which makes you look as if you're dowsing for water with your dog, is to stimulate his nerve endings, a process that can help to rebuild those nerves.

I left Shoemaker's office that day with renewed hope for Hans, a book about communicating with animals through mental imagery, and three additional supplements to add to Hans' food: Canine Corta-FLX Solution™, which contains glucosamine, MSM, and chondroitin; Geri-Form tablets, a vitamin supplement for elderly dogs; and an extract of pig thyroid that was prescribed just in case Hans was hypothyroid.

Hans' mobility was slightly improved after his first visit to Shoemaker. When it was time for his second visit eleven days later, I insisted that my wife leave work early so that she could see this marvelous place and meet this fascinating veterinarian-philosopher who discoursed on the teachings of the Dalai Lama, animals' place in the universe, and all manner of engaging topics as she worked. My wife was as captivated by her visit as I had been.

By December 30, 2000, Hans' seventh birthday, he was standing more frequently, attempting to walk more often, and stringing six or seven steps together before his hind end collapsed and he was obliged to collect himself in order to continue. He was, by then, able to make his way across the kitchen floor, onto the side porch, and down the two steps leading to the driveway. From there we carried him into the yard.

The bad news was that we were still faced with the matter of Hans' incontinence. We tried stud pants and a dainty contraption meant to keep females in heat from soiling the Karastan, but as Hans still dragged himself around a good deal of the time, he could lose his pants quicker than a college freshman during pledge week. We tried wrapping a Depend® around his middle, using tape to keep it secure, but he managed to shed that, too.

Shoemaker had said that Hans should wear a harness instead of a collar, so Mary Ann hit upon the idea of keeping a Depend in place by securing it to the harness with two strips of tape that ran like suspenders from the Depend to the harness and back. That arrangement enabled Hans to reclaim his spot on the bed at night and, as you recall, to attend my birthday party.

Though Hans was under control at night, his waking hours were another story. He continued to urinate, if not at will, at the slightest inspiration.

I am not a patient man, nor can I be called long-suffering. Or short-suffering, for that matter. Thus I muttered more than once after splashing into a Hans puddle, "I don't know how much more of this [crap] I can put up with." That I allowed myself to end a sentence with a preposition testified to my frustration. Further testament to that frustration was the fact that I "decided" more than once that perhaps it was time for Hans to move on to another home or another life.

I never carried out those decisions, although I believe, as I observed to Shoemaker one day, that putting down a crippled dog can be viewed as a kindness because you're freeing him from a broken body so he can take up residence in one that works in his next life. The good veterinarian replied that perhaps there was more that Hans was meant to accomplish in this life.

I'm sure Hans feels that way. Throughout his ordeal he has remained the spirited, eager, uncomplaining, sometimes disobedient, always endearing dog he ever was. One thing he has taught me for sure is that I have a genuine knack for expressing a dog's bladder.

Holding him away from me so as not to get baptized yet again, I squeezed his sides lightly, figuring, as most guys would, that he might as well go for distance in addition to volume.

The seeds of this discovery were sown one day as I lifted Hans up to carry him into the house at dinner time. He began to pee like a racehorse after the Kentucky Derby. Holding him away from me so as not to get baptized yet again, I squeezed his sides lightly, figuring, as most guys would, that he might as well go for distance in addition to volume. When I did, the golden shower he was emitting gained several degrees of arc. Better yet, for the first time in many weeks he didn't pee the floor at mealtime.

For some reason—congenital stupidity perhaps—I didn't see this event as having any practical implications for Hans' day-to-day maintenance until he and I visited Shoemaker a week or so later. After an hour in the office that day, Shoemaker suggested that we "walk" Hans before she rewrapped his tail.

Hans made his way about as usual, sniffing here and sniffing there, but not making the connections necessary to be productive. That was when I remembered the day I had squeezed Hans after picking him up. I said to Shoemaker, "Couldn't you express his bladder and make him pee so we could go back inside?"

"That's a good idea," she exclaimed.

As she was expressing Hans, I asked if it was difficult to do. She said no and explained the process to me. It's surprisingly easy. Even if you've never had occasion to feel a canine bladder at high tide, you'll have no trouble recognizing one. It's slightly smaller than a plum and feels like one of those balls some people squeeze to develop their hand muscles.

Mr. Bladder doesn't always present himself immediately for your inspection, but if you hold one hand steady just above and to the rear of the tip of your dog's squirter while you fish around gently with the other hand, Mr.

If you want to earn extra merit points, you can try writing your dog's name in the snow, but don't let the neighbors observe you during this activity.

Bladder will soon slide between your hands. At this point your dog may squat somewhat, and as soon as you squeeze the good times will begin to roll. Mr. Bladder may attempt to escape before he's completed his work, but your intuition and the way that sucker feels will tell you whether you need to coax him into firing again.

About the only other bits of advice you need to qualify for your merit badge in this activity are these: keep your dog's feet and your shoes out of the way, and don't inhale. If you want to earn extra merit points, you can try writing your dog's name in the snow, but don't let the neighbors observe you during this activity.

After I had become a regular Dr. Goodhands, life improved immensely. A freshly squeezed Hans doesn't pee the floor every time he eats or every time my wife comes home from work. Indeed, a freshly squeezed Hans doesn't pee the floor at all, nor does he soil his Depend at night. As a matter of fact, Hans has become so dependable that we've long since dispensed with suiting him up before bedtime.

We still don't know if Hans will regain control of his personal functions. If the nerves that regulate those functions are dead, he won't be continent again; but if those nerves are merely squashed, Hans might one day regain his self control. That recovery, if it occurs, will be a long time coming, because nerves grow at the rate of only one-eighth to one-quarter of an inch per month.

More than a year has passed since Hans' first visit to Shoemaker, and the changes she wrought in that dog continue to amaze and delight us. He is now able to stand throughout dinner, to turn around without falling, and to walk to and from the yard on his own. Such is his improvement that he hasn't been to see the vet since September 11, 2001.

Politicians and other folks tell us incessantly that life in this country will never be the same after that day, and Hans' life certainly hasn't. I've stopped taking him for acupuncture treatments. Lest you think, however, that I've carried patriotic fervor to truly freakish heights, permit me to recount the Second Miracle of Hans.

About a week after Hans' September 11 visit to Shoemaker, his ability to get around on his own began to deteriorate, and by the end of the month he was no better than he had been the year before. He was reduced to dragging himself around once again, and we began to consider spinal surgery as the cord of last resort. Then, in mid-October, as swiftly as he had regressed, Hans began to stand and to move around on his own. Figuring that the best intervention is sometimes no intervention, I decided there was no point to further acupuncture treatments as long as Hans was getting around so well. I'd miss the long drives to Shoemaker's office and the excuse they provided for going out to lunch, but I've never been one to shirk a sacrifice where my dogs are concerned.

As of this writing, Hans is walking as well as he has at any time since he first went lame seventeen months ago. His nerve endings, like the dog they inhabit, apparently have a mind of their own. Although we are not taking Hans for acupuncture treatments or spinal manipulation at present, we continue to give him his various supplements. Hans, for his part, continues to give us the singular combination of devotion and dogged independence that first drew us to him that frozen winter eight years ago.

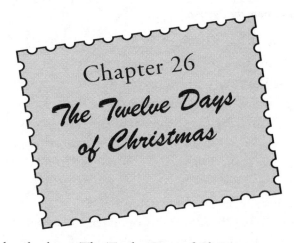

Chapter 26
The Twelve Days of Christmas

Few people who hear *The Twelve Days of Christmas* are aware of the history of this irritating carol; and even those who appreciate that history—Elizabethan scholars, Christmas enthusiasts, and writers working on books about pug dogs—are at odds regarding the carol's origin. Elizabethan scholars maintain that *The Twelve Days of Christmas* evolved in England between 1558 and 1829, an interval during which Catholics were prohibited by law from practicing their faith in public or private. They were even prohibited from being Catholic, for being Catholic in England then was a hanging matter. Consequently, *The Twelve Days of Christmas* was written to help children learn the tenets of the Catholic faith in secret. The two turtle doves, for example, represent the old and the new testaments; the three French hens signify the theological virtues—faith, hope, and charity; the six geese a-laying connote the six days of creation; the ten lords a-leaping are the ten commandments. Whether the lords are leaping in joy or in dismay has never been determined.

Persons devoted to yuletide traditions believe that *The Twelve Days of Christmas* evolved from a French children's game. The foundation for this belief is presented in a book written by Leigh Grant entitled *Twelve Days of Christmas: A Celebration and History*. Ms. Grant reports that the words of *The Twelve Days of Christmas* first appeared in *Mirth without Mischief*, a book published in the early 1780s in England. The melody that traditionally accompanies those words, however, is much older and is thought to have originated in France, where it was part of a memory-and-forfeits game played by children. The leader recited the first verse, the next child recited the second, and the recitation continued until someone missed his or her verse and had to chug a glass of wine.

A third opinion regarding the origin of *The Twelve Days of Christmas* is expressed by people writing books about pugs. This group believes *The Twelve Days of Christmas* was written by Pugnacio (pug-*nay*-tsee-oh) the Elder, a seer, clairvoyant, and mead brewer, who was born in England in 1740. Because of a disagreement with King George III regarding hunting rights, Pugnacio immigrated to Philadelphia in 1775. There he operated the Beer, Bingo, and Brothel tavern, an establishment much favored by the framers of the Constitution who adjourned there after longs days at the quill. Pugnacio owned two pugs and had large portraits of them painted on the doors of his coach. He wrote *The Twelve Days of Christmas* for the benefit of pug owners who could not read and, therefore, were not able to appreciate the horoscopes published in the Philadelphia newspaper.

Pug owners who did not know when they were born could select a Zodiac sign by throwing a handful of pennies or, if they were poor, a handful of ha'pennies twice. The number of heads in a toss determined the sign of the Zodiac. One head is Capricorn, two heads Aquarius, and so on.

The predictions of Pugnacio the Elder are remarkable in their foresight, and because he clearly envisioned a number of modern inventions—the cell phone among them—his horoscopes remain relevant to this day. The following predictions of Pugnacio were written in early December 1775, but they might just as well have been written yesterday. In fact, parts of them were.

Aquarius (1/20–2/18): Theologians, tarot-card readers, and those who forecast the weather have long argued about the significance of the partridge and the pear tree. Most Pugnacio scholars believe the partridge is a symbol of false prosperity, ersatz laughter, and absurdly glowing hair. The pear tree is associated with annoying child actors and loathsome bubble-gum music. These qualities are identified, not coincidentally, with the infamous Partridge family.

"When what to my wondering eyes should appear…"

Pisces (2/19–3/20): Turtledoves are found in several varieties— red, ringed, and laughing among them. Pisces hoping to interpret the turtledove's message should bear in mind that for each prediction, there is an equal and opposite counterprediction. If you pull the lever on the Great Slot Machine of Life and both turtledoves come up laughing, you will either be the laughingstock of your neighborhood or you will win a large sum of money in Las Vegas.

Aries (3/21–4/19): Three French hens bear witness to a refined taste and sensibility. They are also emblematic of a perfectionistic nature and a fascination with prime numbers. Indeed, the number three is often called the number of perfection. There were three wise men, three blind mice, three stooges, and three amigos.

Taurus (4/20–5/20): The four colly birds are an obvious reference to an airborne version of the four horsemen of the apocalypse— Winkin, Blinkin, Nod, and Elton. These winged kamikazes fly lethal missions to terrorize last-minute shoppers. If you must venture out after noon on December 23, wear sturdy headgear and make sure your cell phone battery is charged.

Gemini (5/21–6/21): Five golden rings, to most women, symbolize the capricious state of matrimony, especially in the early twenty-first century. Men, however, interpret these rings as a testimony to the wisdom of having as many players as possible with Super Bowl experience on your fantasy football team.

Cancer (6/22–7/22): The six geese a-laying are a portent of prosperity and, according to some people, a reference to the six days of creation. To more secular types the geese suggest a six pack of a certain intoxicating beverage.

Leo (7/23–8/22): Seven swans a-swimming are a commentary on the cause of the back problems that afflict so many Leos. The swans suggest that back problems are caused by a squishy mattress. Alternately, they suggest the imminent arrival of an invitation to the ballet. Turn it down if you can do so without ruffling any feathers.

Virgo (8/23–9/22): Eight Maids A-Milking are an Ohio-based square dance team whose homogenized image appeals to people who entertain bucolic fantasies about life in a simpler America. If one maid has chocolate milk in her pail, you will get a letter from a long-lost relative soon.

Libra (9/23–10/23): For most people, nine drummers drumming signify an unhealthy interest in militarism, conformity, and martial music. For Libras, however, it's the tenth drummer, commonly known as the different drummer, whose rhythms set the pace for the music in the soul. That drummer's name is Ringo, but his son Zak is a much better player.

Scorpio (10/24–11/21): The ten ladies dancing appear every day from noon until three at Big Al's Cabaret and Lounge in Reading, Pennsylvania—or someplace just like it near you. If more than half the maids are named after herbs and flowers, the groundhog will not see his shadow this year, and the world's financial markets will react accordingly.

Sagittarius (11/22–12/21): The eleven pipers piping are cake decorators, a not-too-subtle reference to Sagittarians' fabled sweet tooth and their tendency to gain weight easily. If your friends chip in and get you a salt lick for Christmas, you'll know its time to lay off the Ben & Jerry's.

Capricorn (12/22–1/19): The twelve lords a-leaping represent the dozens, a vocabulary-building exercise in which participants say vile and detestable things about other participants' mothers. Your verbal acuity makes you a natural at this game, but your tendency to cry easily puts you at a disadvantage in formal competitions.

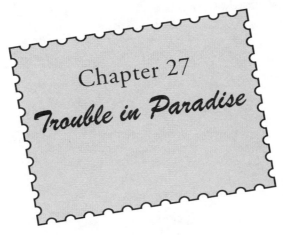

Chapter 27

Trouble in Paradise

And don't go mistaking Paradise
For that home across the road.
Bob Dylan

Our house has a brand new, gleaming "For Sale" sign plunked in the front yard like some cocktail umbrella. I begin to get seller's remorse every time I see that sign—even though it's only a few days old—because once you've plunged a brand new, gleaming "For Sale" sign into your front lawn, Alice doesn't live here any more, and neither do you. You're a working guest in your own bed-and-breakfast, and until the sign is removed by some real estate agent with a prosthetic grin and visions of zeros dancing in her head, you're obliged to take part in the bizarre ritual of washing your clean laundry in public—no mean feat when your house is also home to six pugs and seven cats.

I will miss many things about this stone-and-frame retreat we have occupied for the last seventeen years. I'm especially fond of the screened-in front porch and the two concrete lion statuettes that guard the steps leading to the porch. The lions, whose raiment changes with national holidays and the seasons, are still wearing their bordello-red Halloween masks, but soon they'll don their gay apparel in anticipation of Christmas.

One thing I will not miss is the gnarled, sinister-looking apple tree that stands, cronelike, at the foot of our driveway near the sidewalk. Having lived at the mercy of that crone, I understand how God feels about apple trees; for this tree, Gentle Reader, is one of those Knowledge-of-Good-and-Evil varieties that created all the havoc in the Bible.

Like its celebrated ancestor, the apple tree near the sidewalk at the foot of our driveway spells trouble in paradise. I have told our pugs a thousand times not to eat of the fruit of this cursed tree because it's too close to the street, but they continue to disobey me as if they were all named Adam or Eve.

That's the difference between God and me: he never repeats himself. The other difference is that God gave his tenants the boot (or was it the sandal?) after they had disobeyed him, sentencing them to bear children in pain and to raise them in even greater pain. I don't have those options. First of all, my pugs are altered now. What's more, they've signed me to a series of unbreakable personal service contracts. No matter how vexing their behavior, I'm bound to continue providing the care and feeding to which they've become accustomed. Fortunately, there's nothing in my contract that makes it site-specific; and once that "For Sale" sign comes down, the apple tree will reign over somebody else's parade.

The tree of which I speak is the mother of all apple trees: a crab apple. It produces bitter-tasting, mutated fruit that only pugs, bees, and other hive-dwelling creatures could love in its raw form. The tree was well-established when we moved into this house, but until we acquired our first pugs ten years ago, we had no idea that a tree could inflict so much pain without falling on you.

Our first pug was named Percy, an unfortunate name for a toy dog with no testicles in a small village where you have to own a pickup truck with outsized wheels if you want to get invited to the best barbeques. After we had brought Percy home, we took him outside and showed him the yard, which begins ten or twelve feet to the left of the two steps that lead to our side porch. We also showed him the apple tree, which is located ten yards or so down the driveway to the right of the side-porch steps. We told him he was free to eat the fruit of all the other trees and vines in paradise—namely the walnut tree across the driveway from the side porch and the

During a spirited round of "This Old Man" young Alphonse sneaks off for a potty break.

raspberry canes in the back yard—but he was forbidden to eat the fruit of the apple tree because it was too close to the street.

As Adam had been in Eden, Percy was a model citizen until we gave him a roommate. Before that he showed no inclination to eat the fruit of the apple tree at the foot of the driveway.

Believing that it was not good for a pug to live without the company of his own kind, we brought Debby home about six months after Percy had arrived. We repeated the grand tour of paradise— and the warning about the apple tree—for Debby's benefit. No more than a few days after that, on an otherwise fine summer morning, we took the dogs outside. Instead of turning left and following us the few feet up the driveway to the yard, Debby turned right and headed down the driveway toward the apple tree. Percy turned right with her, as she was the alpha dog. Indeed, Debby would have been the alpha dog in the devil's pack.

As the dogs ambled down the driveway to see what had fallen out of the apple tree, we called them to return, but they ignored us. When they reached the fallen fruit, a couple of sniffs confirmed their hopes that it was edible.

We called the dogs again, and again they ignored us. They were too busy grazing. Though we didn't fully realize it at the time, we were witnessing the canine equivalent of original sin; and as the Bible tells us, the sin of the canine falls on the family.

Despite being more than twenty feet high, the apple tree did not bear much fruit. With a little diligence, which is more diligence than I normally possess, I could have stemmed the dogs' apple fixation by spending a couple of minutes every few days picking up the handful of apples that sporadically fell from the tree. Instead I allowed the dogs their small indulgence, and by mid-October—after they had carried off every apple in sight—they showed no further interest in the tree.

Neither did I, unfortunately. If I had, I might have learned sooner rather than later that crab apple trees have alternate-year flowering and fruiting cycles—a trait they share with my first wife—and I wouldn't have been so dismayed when the tree began to hurl down crabby, gnarled fruit the following summer.

To make matters worse, we had four pugs by then because Debby had borne fruit that year herself; her daughters, Patty and Ella, had joined our pack. Multiply four pugs by four trips outside by four trips back inside each day by the fifty days or so that crab apples are in season, factor in Debby's and Patty's inclination to see what lay beyond the apple tree, and you can understand why I often wished to pave paradise and put up a parking lot.

Living in paradise lost for the last ten years has taught me not only how God feels about apple trees but also how he feels about human nature—ambivalent, the same way I feel about our pugs' regard for apples. As much as I find their cheerful disobedience distressing, I have to smile occasionally at their enthusiasm as they dash toward the apple tree like children bolting through the schoolhouse door the day summer vacation begins. I am also amused by the way in which the differences among the dogs' personalities play out after they've reached the apples.

The most obedient pugs, responding to my third or fourth entreaty, grab an apple, then turn and trot up the driveway, apple in mouth, looking like stuffed pigs on the hoof. The more deliberate pugs sniff one apple after another until they find an entree that's perfectly ripe and ready to be eaten. They don't even let on they've heard me until I've called them half a dozen times at increasing volume. The gourmands in the group fancy the apple leathers—dried-out apples that have been flattened by our car wheels. These dogs have to be escorted back to the yard. I am their shepherd; they shall not want to obey me.

If the dogs are drawn to the apple tree in order to gain the knowledge of Good and Evil, I wish they'd get to the Good part soon. They're already well acquainted with Evil, as I am well acquainted with the biennial fruiting and flowering habits of the crab apple tree. Or so I thought.

This past summer was supposed to be a nonfruiting year for the apple tree. *Nonfruiting* can be taken in its Biblical sense here because instead of producing a light crop of apples during odd-numbered years, the apple tree at the foot of the driveway had taken to producing no fruit at all. I looked forward to the summer of 2001, therefore, the way I used to look forward to summers when I taught school. Imagine my horror when I was sitting on the front porch one day last summer and heard the *kerplunk* of a crab apple hitting the driveway. At first I thought I was having a flashback, but no, there was a hideous crab apple in the drive, looking as innocent as a land mine. Before I could say, "What the [heck's] going on here," another *kerplunk* shattered the afternoon's tranquility.

It wasn't bad enough that the apple tree had set its alarm for the wrong year; it had also set its production switch to *high*. This year's apple crop was operatic in scope. That tree must have sent three thousand apples raining down on my pugs' daily parades to the yard. Nothing in the desultory dog training I had attempted with two of our dogs could have helped to prevent the miseries I suffered.

Thankfully, it is now early November. The surprise apple harvest is over. A reasonable facsimile of peace has been restored to our pug troop movements. Soon we'll be getting calls from the real estate agent warning us that she's on her way over with prospective buyers, every one of whom is sure to ask upon first seeing the pugs, "How do you tell them apart?"

I'm also steeling myself for such witty observations as "Their faces look like they ran into a wall!" followed by the ever-popular, "Are they related?" and "Are they all puppies?"

I will suffer these slings and arrows gladly, however, secure in the knowledge that the apple tree will soon be receding in the rear view mirror of my life. In fact, I may even manage a wry chuckle if the person asking any of those inane questions is the owner of a small dog.

Chapter 28
Send in the Clones

If the artificial is not better than the natural,
to what end are all the arts of life?
John Stuart Mill (1806–1873)

Dog owners do not want for advice. An eager, all-knowing chorus of trainers, breeders, communicators, whisperers, grief counselors, holistic gurus, medicine (wo)men, masseuses, dieticians, and psychiatrists—all driven by the belief that the Lord helps those who help others—waves imploringly from the shelves of bookstores across the United States, where sixty million dogs live and make correctable mistakes in forty million households. No matter what might be ailing any of those sixty million dogs—a prolapsed rectum, a lapsed attention span, or an inclination to run laps around the living room—some earnest savant will gladly explain how to solve the problem.

Despite the zeal of dog experts, dog-owning manuals have the shelf life of endive. For example, eight of the eighteen pug dog manuals listed on Amazon.com were out of print at the time of this writing (June 2003). That circumstance nearly convinced me that all the great pug dog book ideas—as well as the not-so-great ones—had been taken; but then I read about CC, the world's first cloned kitten, and I knew at once that here was an opportunity to go boldly where wise men fear to tread. I resolved to write *The Absolute Complete Dummy's Guide to Cloning and Retraining a Pug Dog.* This resolution was made easier by the fact that I am the author of one of the surviving pug dog manuals, so in order to produce the new book all I'll have to do is clone the old one.

As all dog-care manuals must, *The Absolute Complete Dummy's Guide to Cloning and Retraining a Pug Dog* begins with a brief history of its subject. CC the kitten (the name is short for carbon copy) was re-born in a laboratory at Texas A&M University's College of Veterinary Medicine on December 22, 2001. She was conceived by a team of researchers who extracted body cells from a lab cat named Rainbow, then placed those cells into hollowed-out cat eggs. (A hollowed-out, or enucleated, egg is one from which the nucleus has been removed.) After zapping each egg-cell couplet with an electro-chemical stimulus in order to induce fusion and embryonic cell division, researchers grew the resulting embryos in a culture medium, the ingredients of which need not concern us here. Finally, the embryos were implanted in surrogate cat mothers. This recipe might sound straightforward, but the researchers at Texas A&M needed eighty-seven embryos and eight surrogate mothers in order to produce CC.

For the record, CC was not the first cloned animal. That niche in history belongs to Dolly, a sheep cloned in Scotland in 1996. Since then researchers have also cloned mice, cattle, pigs, goats, and Britney Spears. What makes CC unique is the fact that she is the first cloned companion animal.

Although CC was created in Texas A&M's laboratories, she was not born in a vacuum. She was formulated as part of Operation CopyCat, a research project funded by Genetic Savings & Clone (GSC), a commercial gene bank and animal-cloning enterprise with laboratories and offices in College Station, Texas, and Sausalito, California, and a Web site at www.savingsandclone.com. Anyone interested in cloning a pug can place an order with GSC online or by calling 866-9CLONES (866-925-6637).

Operation CopyCat, for its part, is the offspring of the $3.7 million Missyplicity Project. The latter is dedicated to cloning a Border collie-Siberian husky cross named Missy, who is owned by eighty-two-year-old billionaire John Sperling, founder of the

University of Phoenix. Sperling's $3.7 million contribution to Operation CopyCat led to the creation of CC. That success and another million dollars or so will result, Sperling hopes, in the eventual re-creation of Missy.

In addition to an historical overview, how-to manuals must also present a philosophical—or at least a serious-sounding—discussion of any social questions that pertain to the acquisition and care of a breed. Books about pit bulls, for example, generally mention that they've been known to snack on children.

Consequently, books about cloning should report that most people abhor the idea. According to a May 2001 Gallup poll, 64 percent of Americans favor a ban on animal cloning. Many of them argue that humans have no business "playing God," but this belief is shortsighted. If humans don't play God, somebody else will. Besides, pugs and other pedigreed dogs stopped reproducing by natural selection the minute they became pedigreed, if not sooner. Many pugs do not even breed naturally, unless your idea of natural is a liaison with a turkey baster in somebody's basement. Breeders already practice a crude, inefficient form of cloning known as line breeding. Why not replace that shotgun approach with modern technology?

Other opponents of cloning, most notably the Humane Society of the United States (HSUS), argue that cloning is irresponsible because there are so many homeless animals put to sleep in shelters each year. Does HSUS mean to say that if people willing to fork over thousands of dollars to have their pets cloned were to adopt animals instead, it would put a noticeable dent in pet overpopulation? The presence of unwanted animals in shelters, an unfortunate, lamentable situation, does not constitute a one-size-fits-all moral imperative.

According to protocol, the philosophical discussion in a how-to manual is followed by obligatory warnings. Thus, I should alert you that a cloned animal may not look exactly like its parent. CC, in fact, is tabby-and-white, while Rainbow is a calico. This difference is attributed to a phenomenon called "X-linked inactivation," which is not fully understood by scientists and not understood at all by me. X-linked inactivation means that what you see is not always what you get. If you've done any catalog shopping, you probably have a working notion of this concept.

Apart from looking a bit different from its parent, a cloned animal might also act somewhat differently because temperament is only partially determined by genetics—and there is much disagreement among scientists regarding the extent of that determination. People interested in cloning their pugs, however, should consider this an opportunity, not an obstacle. Anybody who loves a pug well enough to clone it is likely to treat the clone at least as well as the original model was treated. What's more, a clone could have an even better personality than its parent because the owner of the clone isn't apt to repeat any training or disciplinary mistakes he or she might have made with the clone's parent.

Persons considering cloning should also be warned that the process is expensive. GSC, which owns private-sector rights to the cloning technology developed at Texas A&M, has begun offering cat-cloning services at a price in the low six figures. That number, GSC hopes, will eventually be reduced to less than $10,000. Dog cloning, which is more difficult—and, hence, more expensive—than cloning a cat, could be available within a few years.

The first cost in cloning is the fee for collecting and banking genetic material from the parent animal. GSC supplies a DNA deposit kit upon request, but pug owners will have to arrange with a veterinarian to have two small skin samples removed from their dogs under local or general anesthesia. GSC, which cautions that prices will vary from one veterinarian to the next, reports that "the cost for tissue sampling at the Texas A&M Small Animal Clinic ranges from $100 to $700, depending on the condition of the animal." GSC will also help pet owners locate veterinarians who can take tissue samples.

After the veterinarian has taken the samples, he or she forwards them to GSC in a BioBox™ supplied by the company. The samples are grown in a culture medium in GSC's laboratories for as long as a

Did you say "Send in the clowns" or "Send in the clones"?

month before being preserved in liquid nitrogen cold enough to keep a Stauffer's frozen entree until the next millennium, which, as everyone knows, will not begin until 3001. GSC charges $895 (plus $95 for round-trip FedEx delivery in the United States) to store genetic material extracted from a healthy pet for one year. Maintenance storage runs $100 for each additional year. Storage of DNA collected from a dead or dying pet is $1,395 (plus $115 FedEx delivery charges) for one year's storage, and $150 for each additional year.

Obviously, the time to start saving for cloning is when your pug is young. Don't wait until your pug is sick or dying before deciding that you want to have him or her cloned, and don't hesitate to let your friends know that they can support your intention by purchasing a simple gift certificate for you from the GSC Web site. Gift certificates are available in any dollar value, plus a $20 printing-and-shipping charge, which includes FedEx delivery.

Despite its cost, cloning offers many advantages to pug owners beyond allowing them to have their Kates and Ediths too. Genetic diseases could be eliminated through the combined use of cloning and embryo screening. Last year a geneticist in her early thirties who knows she will develop Alzheimer's disease within ten years used embryo screening to select an embryo free from the rare genetic mutation that has triggered the early onset of Alzheimer's in several other members of her family. Nine months later the geneticist gave birth to a "normal" child. Unfortunately, three months later she couldn't remember its name.

Embryo-screening can also be used to select embryos free of other genetic conditions, including breast cancer and Huntington's disease. Perhaps one glorious day pug owners whose favorite pets are carried off by a disease such as pug dog encephalitis will be able to re-create those dogs after first arranging to have the gene(s) responsible for that disease removed from a dog's DNA prior to cloning.

> *As a pug owner, one of my favorite aspects of cloning is the naming possibilities to which it gives rise: Spitting Image, Ditto, Replay, Encore, Deja New, Reflection, George Cloney, and Lazarus.*

As dizzying as the prospects of cloning a favorite pug might be, owners should not forget the advice contained in how-to manuals devoted to pugs produced the old-fashioned way— through artificial insemination. If you're buying a cloned pug, therefore, make sure you see video tapes of the clone's parent, and don't forget to ask for documentation testifying that malicious genes were screened out before cloning took place. Also, ask for documentary proof that the DNA of the clone matches its parent's. And, of course, never buy a puppy from a backyard cloner.

As a pug owner, one of my favorite aspects of cloning is the naming possibilities to which it gives rise: Spitting Image, Ditto, Replay, Encore, Deja New, Reflection, George Cloney, and Lazarus. As a writer I appreciate cloning because it provides an escape hatch from those confining noncompete clauses that publishers use to prevent writers from writing about the same topic for more than one publishing company. Now that the cloned cat is out of the bag, a book such as *Before You Buy That Kitten* can be re-produced as *Before You Clone That Kitten*.

Sensitive to the price considerations surrounding cloning, I plan to provide home cloning kits for each of my books that I decide to clone—beginning with *The Absolute Complete Dummy's Guide to Cloning and Retraining a Pug Dog*. In order to clone this book at home all that readers need to do is Xerox this article, tear a few pages out of the center of the original pug book, stuff the Xeroxed copy of this article into that space, then put the original book in the microwave for fifteen seconds at half power. Let the book stand for two minutes before removing it from the oven.

Chapter 29

Somewhere Over the Rainbow Bridge

Only a fool looking to put a damper on his career would lift a leg on a venerated icon. Consider, for example, John Lennon claiming that the Beatles were more popular than Jesus; Roseanne Barr howling the national anthem and grabbing her crotch before a San Diego Padres game; Sinead O'Connor shredding a photo of Pope John Paul II on "Saturday Night Live." You could get stupid drunk and poke your finger into a nest of paper wasps and you'd stand a better chance of escaping the fallout than these miscreants did.

Apart from showering scorn on popular icons, raising questions about them—even polite, whimsical questions—is the second-best way of ending up with your wit in a wringer. This is no doubt why my father, a man who liked to keep his wits about him, often told me to let sleeping icons lie, especially sleeping dog icons. Yet here I am about to disregard that advice.

"What?!?" I hear a million readers cry. "Is that fool going to claim he's more popular than Scooby Doo? Will he sing 'How Much Is That Doggie in the Window?' then hoist his kit at an SPCA fundraiser? Does he plan to tear up a picture of Air Bud on a local cable show?"

I wish it were that innocent, my friends, but what I'm fixing to do is so colossally thick it might qualify for a Darwin Award. I'm about to raise a few questions regarding the Rainbow Bridge—questions that are bound to get some folks' knickers in a bunch.

I raise these questions knowing full well that in pet society, an infidel who doesn't lower his eyes and voice reverentially whenever the Rainbow Bridge is mentioned is guilty of emotional terrorism. I also know that anybody who questions the Rainbow Bridge concept is doomed to a circle of hell only half a step higher than that reserved for bug-eyed fanatics who detonate Semtex bombs strapped around their waists in crowded dance halls. Finally, I am aware that the guardians of the Rainbow Bridge mythology make John Ashcroft look like Phil Donahue. Therefore, I must advise those readers with a history of heart disease or persistent, unexplainable food allergies in their families to skip to another chapter immediately.

Before the going gets tough, I should explain—for the benefit of the three pet lovers in the continental United States who have not yet heard of it—that the Rainbow Bridge is "a mythical place just this side of heaven where loved pets are made young and healthy again."

That's the Rainbow gospel in a nutshell, as preached by a team of certified animal behaviorists quoted in the *Rocky Mountain News* on January 13, 2003. An unabridged version of that gospel can be found at the Pet Loss Grief Support Web site (www.petloss.com): "When an animal dies that has been especially close to someone…that pet goes to Rainbow Bridge. There are meadows and hills…food, water, and sunshine…our [pets] are warm and comfortable. All the animals who had been ill and old are restored to health and vigor; those who were hurt or maimed are made whole and strong again…The animals are happy and content, except for one small thing; they each miss someone very special to them, who had to be left behind. They all run and play together, but the day comes when one suddenly stops and looks into the distance."

Let us pause at this violin crescendo to ask ourselves what it was that caught Old Yeller's eye. Was it Jesus stomping on a pile of Beatle albums? The pope drawing a mustache on a picture of Sinead O'Connor—who, in 1999, became the first woman to be ordained a priest in the Latin Tridentine Church, a Roman Catholic splinter group with a bishop known throughout Ireland for performing phone-in confessions? If either of those is your final answer, you should have asked Regis if you could call your brother-in-law for an opinion.

What caught Old Yeller's attention—and I'm going to put this as delicately as possible—is his former caregiver gliding on a cloud toward the Rainbow Bridge, draped in designer robes, smiling beatifically, and looking forty pounds and several chins lighter than the last time—or any other time—Old Yeller can remember. After a glorious reunion, Yeller and his caregiver walk gaily over the Rainbow Bridge into heaven, where every day is a great hair day and you never have to wait for a table.

"So what's wrong with that idea?" I hear a million readers ask. "And what's wrong with you, you dung-worshiping chowderhead, for cracking wise about this beautiful, comforting story?"

I wish I knew. I have tried telling myself that the Rainbow Bridge is only a myth and that ever since human beings learned to scratch themselves and walk upright at the same time they have sought comfort in myths. Nevertheless, I am driven by the voice of some inner demon—perhaps the voice of the same black Lab that got David Berkowitz into all that bother—to suggest that myths, though they might not reflect reality, do reflect the mindsets of the people who subscribe to them; and that the mindset of a grieving former pet owner is a terrible thing to which to lay waste.

My questions about the Rainbow Bridge begin with the notion that "loved pets are made young and healthy again." I have no quarrel with 87.5 percent of that idea—in fact, a significant part of my discretionary income is spent on keeping my pets healthy in their present lives—but I have to ask why only "loved" pets qualify for the cosmic makeover.

What about the Shepherd–serial-killer mix chained to a tree in a back yard like a lawn ornament—a dog that isn't allowed to sleep in the house at night and is finally "surrendered" at an animal shelter because he barks too much? If he doesn't get adopted, will he be turned away at the Rainbow Bridge like some geek who shows up at a trendy nightspot in a pair of Wal-Mart jeans? If a meaningful relationship with humans is a prerequisite for admittance to the Rainbow Bridge and, ultimately, heaven, what does that say about the human ego and the underlying assumptions of the human-animal bond?

And what about the feral cat and her newborn kittens—alone, unwanted, and unloved—who die a lingering death outdoors or, if they're lucky, are given a humane exit in an animal shelter? Will they be denied a pass to the Rainbow Bridge because nobody loved them?

I also wonder why pets need a human escort to enter heaven. Is heaven like one of those condominium communities where all the window curtains have to be white and pets aren't allowed to play in their backyards unless they're accompanied by their owners? Why can't animals wait inside heaven for their folks? Are there people in heaven who don't like animals? If so, somebody ought to tighten up on the entrance requirements.

After racking my brain for an answer to these questions, a process that takes about as long as your average Google search, I recalled the wisdom of a dog trainer who warned that we won't have perfect control over our dogs if we allow them to precede us through a doorway without permission. Could this be the theory behind Rainbow Bridge? Is the afterlife the place where our dogs finally come the first time we call them?

Before resting my case and departing for a country that doesn't have an extradition treaty with the United States, I would like to point out that I am not alone in raising questions about the Rainbow Bridge. Witness the following inquiry published by a *Chicago Sun-Times* columnist on April 10, 2001:

"I enjoyed your column about [the Rainbow Bridge]…but I've wondered: What if the [pet] owner dies first? Do you think there's a place where owners frolic and play while waiting for their pets?"

The Dollywood Bridge perhaps? The Branson, Missouri, Bridge? The Great Hugh Hefner Mansion in the sky?

This who-goes-first question is not the final hanging chad on the Rainbow Bridge tally sheet, either. Many people, including me, own several pets in a lifetime. Indeed, I have six pugs and seven cats presently, all of whom I bid fair to outlive—so long as I don't

The infamous Ma Barker knew from an early age that she was destined for shortness.

continue writing offensive material like this. Yet what if I predecease some of my current pets? Will I be obliged to wait at the Rainbow Bridge with my former pets, listening to the sounds of the heavenly choir wafting from across the bridge, until all my surviving pets have died? If so, I hope the bridge has digital cable, broadband Internet access, and good Asian restaurants. Moreover, what if I, as some of you may suspect, don't have the board scores or the references to get into heaven? What becomes of my pets then?

Or what happens if an animal's owner dies, the animal gets adopted by a person to whom that animal also becomes attached, and then the animal dies? With which owner does the animal live happily ever after? Are there custody fights at the Rainbow Bridge? A family court with some television or celebrity judge presiding?

Obviously, the Rainbow Bridge is a myth in need of a codicil. As a matter of fact, for people who believe in reincarnation—as one in four Americans do, according to an October 2001 Gallup poll—

the Rainbow Bridge is in need of a regime change. Those who believe in reincarnation—a heroic act of faith given the horrors of first grade and first marriages—contend that the spirits animating our pets live on after their bodies have worn out, either returning to Earth in a new body or becoming one with the Tao.

Be that as it may, I have difficulty understanding why an animal's spirit, especially a pug's, should be subject to an extended wait command in the sky simply to help ameliorate human grief. I am more disposed to think that the animating spirit in pugs and other four-legged creatures returns to this world in the form of another being. In the case of pugs, that would be another pug, because pugs are already the highest form of life.

I would like to say more, but the folks from the witness protection program are here. Before I go, I apologize if I have offended anyone by suggesting that the Rainbow Bridge sounds like a Disneyland rest stop without the leash regulations. I would make a public confession of my sins, but the boys in witness protection advise against it. I will have to make do, I suppose, with phoning in my mea culpas to Sinead O'Connor's bishop at 1-800-CON-FESS.

Chapter 30
Bonus Track (CDs Have 'em. Why Not Books?)

Time is a great teacher,
but unfortunately it kills all its pupils.
Hector Berlioz

The pugs and I are getting along in years. Hans, the eldest, is nine; his half-sister June, whom I often refer to as my dog wife, is eight; her sons, Burt and Harry, are six-and-a-half; and I turned sixty in January (2003). No matter how we cut the cards—in dog, human, or metric years—none of us is playing with a full deck. Only Fetch and Dexter, whom we adopted four years ago when they were both roughly ten months old, can be said to be in the bloom of youth. For the rest of us, the bloom is several shades paler than it was at its peak—and is looking rather dog-eared to boot. Granted, the road still rises up to meet us most of the time, but one day it will rise up only because we have toppled forward onto our faces.

I worry increasingly about that day. The slightest twinge in the upper left quadrant of my body is enough to make me fear that "the big one" is at hand. Instead of checking the sports scores first thing in the morning, I check my blood-sugar level and the obituaries to see if I'm still alive. I show up for doctors appointments without having to be subpoenaed. At least once a month I vow to give up red meat, white meat, the other white meat, coffee, eggs, dairy products, soft drinks, hard drinks, and chemical additives. I have started using filtered water for cooking as well as drinking. Indeed, I'd use filtered water to brush my teeth and to take showers if I thought there were any health benefits to be had thereby. Such is my preoccupation with longevity—or shortgevity, in my case—that the other day when I was in a restaurant and the waitress asked if there was anything else she could get me, I said, "Twenty more years would be fine."

"That's the length of my entire life," she replied. I wanted to cry. Instead I took comfort in telling her the worst was yet to come.

Actually, as Woody Allen once said, I'm not afraid of dying, I just don't want to be there when it happens. Moreover, it's not dying that worries me so much as the thought of what occurs afterward. Most accounts of heaven make it sound like a hootenanny at the Betty Ford Clinic on a Sunday night—and the only way to get there is in a hearse. Reincarnation is somewhat cheering—coming back is my only chance of repeating some of my favorite sins—but what if I came back as a person with no sense of irony? Or with six kids instead of six dogs?

Hell, of course, does not figure into my calculations. Several years ago I bought a Deathbed Conversion policy from Repent Life and Casualty after seeing Ed McMahon talking up the company on television. I display my policy in a guilt-edged frame above the bed. In the space where it says *beneficiary*, I wrote *me*. I selected Repent Life and Casualty because I like its motto: "The afterlife you save may be your own."

Although I fear that every unexpected knock at the door might be a delivery person from the Grim Reaper's Take-Away come to present me with my last meal, the pugs remain blissfully unaware of the passage of time—in the global sense. They can always tell to the millisecond how much time has elapsed since their last meal, but they—and all other animals, we are told—are not aware of the passage of time in the larger context. Hence they cannot be faulted for not remembering birthdays or anniversaries. Nor can pugs contemplate their own deaths. If they get a twinge in the upper left quadrants of their bodies, they scratch it and go back to sleep.

This is why the older my pugs and I become, the more I envy them. When they look into a mirror, they don't notice the tracks left by the Armies of Encroaching Age. If pugs walk into a room and

June—whose motto is "Don't leave home without me!"—has more frequent-rider miles than any other pug on the bus.

can't remember what it was they went there to get, they don't curse the dying of the light; they just scratch themselves and lie down. They'll never spend a day in a nursing home; they won't have to put up with senior-moment jokes from their friends; they won't have to contend with Brillo® pads growing out of their ears; no one will ever take a picture of their navels from the inside; and they won't have to go to anyone's funeral.

Pugs are also spared the knowledge of such monstrosities as Older Americans Month, which is "celebrated" each May. I've got news for the folks who thought that one up: getting old is nothing to celebrate. The only thing worse than being an aging youth is being an aging old person. Besides, I find it difficult to get excited about a month that has also been designated National Arthritis Month, National Osteoporosis Prevention Month, National Better Hearing and Speech Month, National Electrical Safety Month, National Bike Safety Month, National Mental Health Month, and National Skin Cancer Awareness Month. If you judge a month by the company it keeps, May is a dodgy character with creaky bones and bad skin who is apt to electrocute himself while joyriding on his stairlift.

The good news, however, doesn't stop there. May is also National Home Remodeling Month. (Modernize that spare room! Send granny to a nursing home!)

As I noted earlier, one of the chief differences between pugs and people is the fact that pugs cannot contemplate their own deaths. That explains why some pugs will stand up to much bigger dogs: what you can't contemplate, you don't fear—nor can you be faulted for not being decently dressed when the uncontemplated happens.

We humans, on the other hand, know the party will be over one day, and we are told that we ought to be prepared for that day's arrival. My first thought was to seek out one of those grief counselors, but that struck me as self-centered—and as an exercise in premature matriculation—so I took out the Deathbed Conversion policy instead. For some reason, though, I still didn't feel sufficiently prepared for the time when a spectral voice will whisper, "Your ride's here." Then one day while I was sitting in a supermarket with my left arm in the cuff of one of those free-blood-pressure-reading machines, it hit me: no one is truly prepared for death who hasn't written his or her obituary.

There is no arguing that an obituary is the most important statement about a person, yet few people devote to their obituaries the attention they deserve. Such neglect is puzzling. Couples spend a great deal of time crafting their wedding vows, and marriage, as we all know, does not always last. Death does. Therefore, an obituary should be a lovingly molded statement.

Unfortunately, that is seldom the case. As anyone who reads obituaries knows, most of them sound like the work of amateurs or low-paid staff writers, at best. How tragic. The thought of dying is only somewhat more disturbing than the thought of one's obituary being written by a stranger who isn't attuned to the nuances of language or—worse yet—who splits infinitives. I'm used to splitting hairs and checks—and the occasional splitting hangover—but I never split infinitives.

My mother got around the obituary dilemma by specifying in her will that she did not want an obituary. Neither did she have a viewing or a public funeral. She must have been furious with someone to whom she did not want to give the satisfaction of knowing she had croaked. At first I thought Mother's approach was a perversely swell idea; then I realized that if a writer died without an obituary, people might think he had died of writer's block, a condition known as dying tabula rasa.

Consequently, after the blood-pressure cuff in the supermarket had released its death grip on my arm, I realized that I wouldn't know true peace until I had composed my obituary. I rushed home, cleared my calendar for the rest of the day—unlike nature, I adore a vacuum—and went to work. I am proud to present the fruits of my labors below. Remember, you read it here first.

Throughout his life, Phil Maggitti defied expectations. His father expected him to be a priest; his mother expected him to heal the sick; his seventh grade teacher expected him to spend most of his adult life in jail; his basketball coach expected him to pass the ball occasionally; his friends expected him to return their calls; and his editors expected him to meet deadlines.

Mr. Maggitti, an only child and happy to be one, displayed a facility with words at an early age. He wrote battle reports in a wry, faux-Hemingway style describing the encounters between the plastic cowboys and Indians that were the playmates of his youth. His devoted mother encouraged the development of his narrative voice by taping pull quotes from his reports on the refrigerator. His working-class father, upon going to the refrigerator for a snack one evening and encountering, "Smoke rose from the campfire in a seductive dance," remarked testily, "That boy needs to spend more time playing outdoors."

After a sylvan interlude in a prep school where the more verbally adroit students were excused from gym class to pursue advance-placement studies, Mr. Maggitti took a degree in English at St. Joseph's University in Philadelphia. There he acquired a love for trench coats, F. Scott Fitzgerald, the serial comma, and foreign films. Upon graduating, he taught English in junior high school for ten years, often referring to himself as "the foreign language teacher."

A profound dislike for children and the inability to function in groups larger than one led Mr. Maggitti to court a solitary muse. During his most productive writing years—1980 to 2000—he wrote eight books and more than eight hundred articles. His work celebrated animals, whose company he preferred to that of most people. His Postcards from the Pug Bus, *a charming collection of anecdotes and reflections inspired by his beloved pugs, is destined to be a classic.*

In addition to being one of the most lucid, witty, and engaging prose stylists of his day, Mr. Maggitti was a splendid, if ruthless, editor. After he had rewritten everything but the author's name in one magazine article he had been given to edit, the "author" complained that she could no longer hear her voice in the piece. Mr. Maggitti promptly replied, "That isn't your voice, madam, it's the wind whistling through your head."

As Mr. Maggitti was an inveterate nonjoiner, his estate requests that in lieu of donations to worthy causes, people should send back anything they have borrowed from him—or a check in the amount of that item's current fair market value. You know who you are, and so do his executors.

Armed with my Deathbed Conversion policy and script approval on my obituary, I am able to rest easier at night. Nevertheless, I still believe that only the paranoid survive, so I will take one final precaution.

I have never bought that nonsense about everyone's death diminishing me. We are all in this alone. I strongly suspect, however, that my own death will diminish me greatly. Therefore, when the bell does toll for me, I'm going to let my answering machine pick up—and it's going to be set for "announcement only."